Praise for Susan Nolen-Hoeksema and *Women Conquering Depression*

"One of the nation's leading authorities on women and depression."

—*USA Today*

"An astute analysis with useful recommendations for change."
—*Psychology Today*

"Susan Nolen-Hoeksema offers young women like myself new ways to understand their pain in clear, unpatronizing language. Most important, her book describes pragmatic tools to heal."

—COURTNEY E. MARTIN, author of *Perfect Girls, Starving Daughters*

"Provocative . . . Nolen-Hoeksema helps readers make sense of their past experiences and the genetic influences, . . . leading to a better understanding of their behavior."

—*Publishers Weekly*

"A brilliant and eminently practical book . . . Nolen-Hoeksema helps those who suffer tap into a wellspring of positive energy."
—WILLIAM S. POLLACK, PH.D., author of *Real Boys*

Women Conquering Depression

WOMEN CONQUERING DEPRESSION

How to Gain Control of Eating, Drinking, and Overthinking and Embrace a Healthier Life

SUSAN NOLEN-HOEKSEMA, PH.D.

A HOLT PAPERBACK

HENRY HOLT AND COMPANY ▲ NEW YORK

In memory of Catherine Nolen

Holt Paperbacks
Henry Holt and Company, LLC
Publishers since 1866
175 Fifth Avenue
New York, New York 10010
www.henryholt.com

A Holt Paperback® and 🅗 ® are registered trademarks
of Henry Holt and Company, LLC.

Distributed in Canada by H. B. Fenn and Company Ltd.

Library of Congress Cataloging-in-Publication Data

Nolen-Hoeksema, Susan, date.
Women conquering depression : how to gain control of eating, drinking,
and overthinking and embrace a healthier life / Susan Nolen-Hoeksema.
p. cm.
Includes bibliographical references and index.
ISBN: 978-0-8050-9222-6
1. Women—Mental health.   2. Depression in women.   3. Eating disorders in women.
4. Women—Alcohol use.   5. Alcoholism—Treatment.   6. Women—Psychology.
I. Title.

RC451.4.W6N64 2006
616.85'27'0082—dc22   2005046087

Henry Holt books are available for special promotions and premiums.
For details contact: Director, Special Markets.

Originally published in hardcover in 2006 by Henry Holt and Company
under the title *Eating, Drinking, Overthinking*

First Owl Books Edition 2007

First Holt Paperbacks Edition 2010

Designed by Victoria Hartman

Printed in the United States of America

1   3   5   7   9   10   8   6   4   2

Contents

P R E F A C E

▼

WOMEN'S MENTAL HEALTH has been my focus and my passion for over twenty years. I've spent the bulk of my career researching and publishing articles on women's mental health in the scientific literature. In 2003, I first translated that research for the general public in *Women Who Think Too Much: How to Break Free of Overthinking and Reclaim Your Life.* In that book I described the phenomenon of overthinking, in which women become trapped in ruminations about the past, the present, and the future that can immobilize them and send them into the depths of depression.

In the few years since I wrote *Women Who Think Too Much,* I have become increasingly concerned with the broader picture of women's mental health and well-being. Overthinking and depression are indeed common and debilitating problems among women, but they are not the only ones. Depression rarely occurs in a vacuum. Instead, as my research has found, it usually occurs alongside other symptoms, and these often involve food or alcohol.

Depressive symptoms, unhealthy eating habits, and heavy drinking can unite to create a space so poisonous for women that I have called it the *toxic triangle*. Women enter the toxic triangle on many different pathways: some by way of depressive symptoms that they try to smother in food or drown in alcohol; some by way of crazy dieting or binge eating, which tears down their self-esteem, sending them plummeting into depression or alcohol abuse; and others by way of drinking, either to please a man or to ease stress, though it appears to set women up for depression and yo-yo eating patterns.

Women Conquering Depression will help you understand your own relationship to the toxic triangle. This book is not just for women who are already aware that they suffer from clinical depression, diagnosed eating disorders, or alcoholism. It is for those who dance around the edges of the toxic triangle, with moderate symptoms of depression, unhealthy eating patterns, or moderate to heavy patterns of drinking. My research shows that there are millions of women who engage in this dance over the course of their lives. Unfortunately, my research also shows that even mild symptoms of depression, eating disorders, or alcohol abuse—not to mention the confluence of all three—can be toxic to women's mental well-being, their physical health, their relationships, and their careers. When the three elements of the toxic triangle intersect, women are pulled into a vortex of misery and self-destruction so powerful that they can find it very difficult to escape.

Escape is possible, however, and I will show you ways out of the toxic triangle. By transforming the very traits that make women vulnerable to the toxic triangle into strengths, we can pull ourselves out. Just as women are extraordinarily sensitive to our own emotions and the emotions of others, and deeply concerned about our relationships, we recognize that these traits can get us into trouble. This is because they so often lead us to engage in what I call *self-focused coping:* handling stressful situations by turning inward on ourselves rather than outward in an attempt to change the situation. Women's emotional and interpersonal sensitivities can, however, be harnessed to create more effective and healthy ways of coping with stress. *Women Conquering Depression* will give you the tools to do this.

If you are a loved one or friend of a woman caught in the toxic triangle, this book will help you understand this deadly space, and how to help her escape it. In the final chapter, I discuss how we can start this effort early by helping girls and young women avoid the pathways that lead into the toxic triangle.

Women Conquering Depression raises an alarm by revealing that the intersection of depression, unhealthy eating, and heavy drinking is as common in women as it has commonly been ignored by both scientists and the lay public. This book also gives hope to women caught in the triangle, as well as to their family and friends, that freedom from the toxic triangle is within our reach.

Women Conquering Depression

ONE

The Toxic Triangle

For Jill, a thirty-year-old account executive at a large bank, there were two distinct parts to each week. When she was "on-duty," from Monday morning to Thursday night, she tightly controlled everything she ate and drank. Breakfast, if she ate it at all, was just a piece of toast with a bit of jam (no butter) and lots of black coffee. Lunch was always a small, pristine salad with no-cal dressing. Dinner was as sparse and low-fat as she could make it and still call it dinner—usually just a frozen diet entree. And alcohol never passed her lips while on-duty, no matter how much she wanted it. Even if she went out with clients to a nice restaurant, she ordered sparkling water, adopting an air of casual self-righteousness about her abstinence from alcohol.

By Thursday night, however, Jill's cravings for food and

drink were powerful. The sense of control and superiority that she gained from avoiding food and alcohol all week were overcome by feelings of frustration, longing, and defeat. Why wasn't she more fulfilled in her job? Could she really handle the stresses of her position? When was she ever going to find a man she could really fall in love with? And why did she have to deprive herself all the time just to stay skinny and put in long hours at work?

The second phase of Jill's week, when she was "off-duty," usually began slowly, on Thursday night. She'd come home from work, feeling tired but agitated, desperately wanting a drink. "Just one drink," she told herself, "I deserve it the way this week has gone." She'd pour herself a glass of sauvignon blanc and sip it slowly while she sorted through mail and microwaved her dinner. "Oh damn," she'd say, when the first glass was drained. "I'm not ready to eat yet." Then she'd pour another glass, vowing that two was going to be her max, for sure. By the time dinner was ready and the second glass was empty, Jill was ravenous. And a diet entree out of the microwave was not what she wanted. She put the entree in the fridge and brought out the chips. "I need some starch to soak up this wine," she'd tell herself. Jill then took her chips, and another glass of wine, and flopped down on the couch to watch TV. It felt so good, such a relief, to let go and do what her mind and her body seemed to want to do—eat and drink. Jill spent the rest of Thursday night snacking on junk food and leftovers and drinking more wine, until she collapsed into bed around midnight.

Of course, she felt terrible the next morning. But Fridays were usually absent of meetings, so she could hole up in her office, popping Advil while kicking herself for her indulgences the night before.

By Friday night, however, she was ready to party. It was the weekend, she was off-duty, and she wasn't going to waste a minute of it. From Friday's happy hour with workmates through a party on Saturday night, into Sunday's get-together with friends to watch football, Jill raged. She ate anything she wanted to—hamburgers and fries, fettuccine Alfredo, everything that she forbade herself while she was on-duty during the week. And she drank. Hard liquor, beer, wine, whatever was being served.

Come Monday morning, Jill was back "on-duty," wracked with self-loathing and shame. Why did she do this to her body? She had to stop, she had to be better about controlling her eating and drinking. She felt dirty, defective, diseased.

JILL ISN'T DISEASED but she has entered a perilous zone where millions of women every year find themselves trapped. This *toxic triangle* is the intersection of three troubles that affect women at alarming rates: yo-yo eating, heavy drinking, and self-criticism and despair. Each of these afflictions does damage on its own. Binge eating and self-starvation ravage a woman's body, increasing her risk of a number of serious diseases. Heavy drinking can wreck a woman's relationships, her career, and her vital organs. Low self-esteem, sadness, and lethargy can stop us in our tracks, preventing us from claiming all that life can provide.

Millions of women play at the edges of depression, eating disorders, and alcohol abuse. They'll take a few steps into the realm of eating disorders, calling their self-deprivation a diet or throwing up a meal every now and then because it "didn't settle right" with them. They'll experiment with how much they can drink before they begin to slur their words. They'll allow themselves a day or two in bed, wallowing in angry thoughts about themselves and others, or just shutting down and not thinking about anything.

These little forays can be insidious. At first, we step over the line just a bit, and pull back relatively quickly. But we are lured to return. The symptoms can feel good—it's such a relief to let go and binge or give up and curl into a little ball. After a while, we find ourselves inside the danger zone for eating disorders, or alcohol abuse, or depression, only this time more often, and for longer. Our symptoms, which were once mild and occasional, have become moderate and more frequent.

More dangerous than either of these discrete realms, however, is their intersection—the toxic triangle. Depressive symptoms, crazy eating habits, and heavy drinking rarely happen independently. As many as 80 percent of women who are drawn into one of these afflictions find themselves crossing the line into at least one of the others. The vortex where all three intersect is a whirling mass of confusing and self-damaging actions and feelings. A woman stuck in the toxic triangle can shift from immobilizing sadness to strength gained from controlling her eating, to shame and frustration from losing that control, and then to the relief of anesthetizing herself through alcohol or binge eating. Her family members and friends may try to help, though the target for their interventions keeps shifting. One day she won't get out of bed, can't get to work, and her voice is pure misery. The next day she seems happier, but she might be drinking heavily. Later, she swears she's stopped drinking, but she's losing (or gaining) weight rapidly.

Why Don't We Recognize the Toxic Triangle?

Although the toxic triangle is both poisonous and prevalent in women's lives, it has been largely ignored both by the lay public and by mental health professionals. One reason is the expectation that mild or moderate symptoms of depression, eating disorders, or alcohol abuse are "typical" for women today, and not terribly dangerous.

We comfort ourselves by saying things like, "Sure I drink, but I'm not a heavy drinker," or "Every woman I know goes on and off diets all the time—I'm no different from them," or "I'm not happy with how my life is going, but I'm not depressed—depression is an illness that you have to take Prozac to get over."

A critically important finding in my own research and other recent studies is that moderate, or subclinical, forms of eating disorders, alcohol abuse, and depression are each in themselves highly toxic and dangerous. These subclinical symptoms chip away at a woman's physical and mental health, harm her ability to function in everyday life, and set her up for more serious symptoms down the road.

Another reason that the toxic triangle has gotten too little attention is that it's just easier to focus on one problem at a time. Scientists tend to study depression *or* eating disorders *or* alcoholism, but rarely do they study two or more disorders at a time. We also like to think linearly—that one thing causes another, and then another, and so on. So if a person is suffering from two or more problems, we tend to think that one must have caused the other. In particular, mental health professionals and laypeople often assume that if a woman is both depressed and binge eating or binge drinking, then the depression must be causing her to binge. This is sometimes the case, but not always. Often the binge eating or binge drinking comes before the depression. And relieving a woman's depression through treatment doesn't automatically stop her from bingeing on food or alcohol.

The toxic triangle is not as simple as one thing causing another. It is a place where symptoms of depression, eating disorders, and alcohol abuse play off one another and enhance one another. There are many pathways into the toxic triangle. Some women enter through the path of depression; others through binge eating and self-deprivation; still others through alcohol. Once they are in the toxic triangle, women can find it very difficult to escape.

Taking It upon Ourselves:
Women's Tendency toward Self-Focused Coping

At the root of women's vulnerability to the toxic triangle is their tendency to respond to stress with what I call *self-focused coping*. When women are faced with a difficult situation, they turn inward to control or change themselves rather than focusing outward on the environment and individuals that need to change. Whereas men tend to externalize stress—blaming other people for their negative feelings and difficult circumstances—women tend to internalize it, holding it in their bodies and minds. When something bad happens to women, they analyze everything about the problem—how they feel about it, why it came about, and all its meanings and ramifications for themselves and their loved ones. Women are acutely aware of how their body feels in reaction to a problem—tension, agitation, lethargy, and a sense of being out of control in reaction to a problem. As a result, they are especially likely to do something to change how their body feels.

Many women do self-destructive and damaging things to overcome their feelings. They may binge eat to escape their feelings in the fleeting pleasures of excess or their favorite "forbidden foods." They may refuse to eat, welcoming the feelings of power and control that come with self-denial. They may drink alcohol or take sedatives in an attempt to anesthetize their feelings. Or they may simply remain glued to their feelings and thoughts, rehashing things that have happened in the past, worrying about what will happen in the future, immobilized by a crushing sense of being overwhelmed.

Self-focused coping takes many forms, but each involves managing your internal self in a misguided attempt to manage external situations. Feeling that you can't do anything about your problems at the moment, you turn inward and focus on how you feel or think about the problems themselves. Not all forms of self-focused coping are self-destructive. Employing strategies to quell your anxiety—such as deep-breathing exercises—can help you think more clearly and is a highly adaptive form of self-focused coping.

But when self-focused coping involves hurting your body in some way, or gets in the way of doing something productive to overcome your problems, it becomes dangerous and maladaptive. Indeed, it can help transport you into the toxic triangle— depression, yo-yo eating habits, and heavy drinking. Self-focused coping can lead to depression by amplifying feelings of despair and preventing you from taking action to overcome the true sources of your problems. Self-focused coping can lead to symptoms of eating disorders by causing you to focus on your control (or lack of control) over your body rather than on the ways you can change your life situation. And self-focused coping can lead to abuse of alcohol and other drugs as a way of escaping those troubling thoughts and feelings that it inspires.

Unfortunately, once a woman enters the toxic triangle, the symptoms of depression, disordered eating, and heavy drinking work in lockstep, creating a self-perpetuating syndrome that grows in intensity. Depression leads to attempts at escape, and many women achieve this through drinking or binge eating. But binge eating and drinking lead to more depression. In fact, the cycling of bingeing and drinking changes the way the body metabolizes food and alcohol. Once the cycling starts, it fuels itself, making it hard to stop.

Women can break out of the toxic triangle. This book will help you understand how the toxic triangle emerges in women's lives and will help you use this knowledge to break free from the power it exerts over your life. Women's self-focusing tendencies develop in part because we are attuned to our own emotional lives and the emotions and needs of others. These sensitivities can be used to acknowledge and understand the sources of our stress, and develop more effective ways of dealing with stressors. Stress need not be internalized or taken out on our bodies and minds; instead, we can learn how to use self-focusing skills to develop the kinds of solutions that strike a balance between our own values and the best interests and needs of those we care about.

The Three Pathways into the Toxic Triangle

Each of the three pathways that lead to the toxic triangle has unique characteristics that draw in its victims. To give you a sense of how each pathway looks and feels, and how each converges into an overpowering trap, I will describe them for you here.

"I JUST DON'T CARE ANYMORE"

Depression has been called "the common cold of modern times."[1] Indeed, rates of depression appear to have increased in recent generations. Researchers Myrna Weissman and the late Gerald Klerman of Columbia University examined data from several studies and determined that people born in the latter part of the twentieth century are much more likely to experience depression than those born in the early part of the century.[2] Lots of different explanations for this generational effect have been offered: older people simply may not remember their periods of depression and so don't report having experienced it, or something about our contemporary life—lack of strong family and social ties, a vacuum of common values, materialism—may be making people, particularly young people, more vulnerable to depression.

Just what is meant by depression? It's a word that is used so casually these days, like *stress,* that it's understood to mean any general feeling of malaise and psychic discomfort. But psychologists and psychiatrists have a specific set of symptoms that they place under the label of depression.

Sadness is the cardinal emotional symptom of depression. You're blue, feel as if you've lost something, as if there's a huge weight on your psychological shoulders. Some people who are depressed don't so much feel sad but it's more like their emotions have been sucked dry and they can't feel anything anymore. What used to give them pleasure now just lands like a dull thud on their consciousness. They watch a favorite movie—one that used to make them smile every time they saw it—and they can't see or hear what used to make them feel so good. They talk with a trusted friend, and instead of feeling relieved or uplifted, they feel dull and drab and lifeless. They go shopping, or go out to eat, and nothing can pique their interest. They really couldn't care less about anything.

The physical symptoms of depression are often confusing because they can swing from one extreme to the other. When you are depressed, you may want to sleep all the time, or you may not sleep at all. You may feel tired, slowed down, heavy, and lethargic, or agitated and unable to sit still.

When you are depressed, your thoughts may be filled with themes of self-blame, guilt, and pessimism. You may feel as though you can't think at all—your powers of concentration and attention have disappeared, along with your ability to make decisions. Writer and researcher Kay Redfield Jamison has described these feelings this way: "It seemed as though my mind has slowed down and burned out to the point of being virtually useless."[3]

One in four women, at some time in her life, will experience symptoms of depression severe enough for a diagnosis of major depression, one of the most severe forms of depression.[4] Milder symptoms of depression, short of such a psychiatric diagnosis, but still painful, plague most women at least occasionally. In one of my own studies, I assessed depressive symptoms in approximately 1,300 adults, half of them women, half men. These people had not sought help for depression or any other psychological problem—they were a random sample of people from all walks of life. Over a third of the women reported experiencing five or more symptoms of depression at the time of the study. Although this may seem like an astonishingly high rate of depressive symptoms, it is well in line with other studies of the general population in the United States, Europe, Australia, and New Zealand.

Women's vulnerability to depressive symptoms seems to skyrocket in early adolescence, as psychologist Jean Twenge of San Diego State University and I showed in another recent study. Employing what is called a *meta-analysis*, we combined data from over 300 studies of depressive symptoms in children and adolescence to examine the emergence of depressive symptoms in girls and boys over time. We found that before about age 13, girls and boys are equally likely to have symptoms of depression, but around age 13 to 15, girls' levels of symptoms escalate sharply, while boys' levels remain relatively flat and even seem to peter out a bit.

While depression is the most familiar pathway into the toxic triangle, there are other ways of getting there. In women, depression rarely occurs by itself; most often, it's accompanied by behaviors that allow a woman to escape depression for a short time, only to ultimately feed and expand the depression further.

"I SHOULDN'T HAVE EATEN THAT"

Do the following statements sound terribly familiar?

> I think my stomach is too big.
> I eat when I am upset.
> I stuff myself with food.

I think about dieting.

I think that my hips are too big.

I feel extremely guilty after overeating.

I am terrified of gaining weight.

If I gain a pound, I worry that I will keep gaining.

I eat or drink in secrecy.

I feel fat even when others say I look thin.

I am very conscious of even small changes in my weight.

I have gone on eating binges when I felt that I could not stop.

Psychologist Peter Lewinsohn of the Oregon Research Institute and his colleagues asked a sample of 1,056 young adults to say how often they had these thoughts about food and their body.[5] It probably won't surprise you to learn that women entertained thoughts of this kind much more often than men did. Many women, perhaps even a majority, spend an inordinate amount of their lives concerned about their weight, what they have and have not eaten, and what they can or cannot eat. Binge eating and excessive dieting are rampant, with 32 percent of college-age women saying they binge at least twice a month and 45 percent of women saying they are chronically on a diet.

Emotional turmoil is especially likely to lead women to eat, binge, and be preoccupied with their bodies. In one of my own studies, I asked young women (25 to 35 years old) and middle-aged women (45 to 55 years old) how they cope when they are sad, blue, anxious, or generally distressed. One of the most common responses of the young and middle-aged women in the study was "I eat." One in four young adult women and one in three middle-aged women say that eating—chocolate and other sweets, chips, anything they can get their hands on—is what they often or always do when they are upset. A smaller but still significant fraction of these women (14 percent of the young adult women and 16 percent of the middle-aged women) say they binge eat when they are upset.[6]

Just as in depression, obsessions about weight, body shape, and dieting begin early in life. Over 70 percent of girls have been on a diet by age 10.[7] Once puberty hits, girls are especially unhappy with their bodies, particularly if they enter puberty a year or so before their girlfriends.[8] They say they feel fat and don't look like the girls in the fashion magazines. Because girls' self-esteem is often closely tied to their figure and weight, their feelings about themselves can take an abrupt turn toward the negative at this age. As a result, they may rely on excessive dieting to try to control their weight.

For some women, concerns about eating and weight become so overwhelming and patterns of eating, or avoiding eating, so out of control that they are said to have eating disorders. This is where a student of mine, whom I'll call Hillary, found herself.

Hillary was always an overachiever. A straight-A student in high school, she was also an extraordinary violinist, playing recitals and concerts to large crowds since she was ten. She began college when she was just seventeen.

The thing Hillary was best at, however, was dieting. At 5 feet 11 inches, she weighed 102 pounds. She began dieting when, in fifth grade, her height soared above her classmates' and she began to feel "big." During her junior year in high school, she decided she had to take drastic measures to lose more weight. She began by cutting her calorie intake by half. She lost several pounds, but not fast enough for her liking, so she cut her intake to 500 calories per day. She also began a vigorous exercise program of cross-country running. Each day, Hillary would not let herself eat until she had run at least ten miles. Then she would have just a few vegetables and a handful of Cheerios. Later in the day, she might have some vegetables and some fruit, but she would wait until she was so hungry that she was faint. Hillary dropped to 110 pounds and she stopped menstruating. Her mother expressed some concern about how little Hillary was eating, but since her mother tended to be overweight, she didn't discourage Hillary from dieting.

When it came time to go to college, Hillary was excited but also frightened, because she wasn't sure she could maintain her straight A's. In the first examination period at college, Hillary got mostly A's but one B. She felt very vulnerable, like a failure who was losing control. She was also unhappy with her social life, which, by the middle of the first semester, was going nowhere. Hillary decided that things might be better if she lost more weight, so she cut her food intake to two apples and a handful of Cheerios each day. She also ran at least fifteen miles each day. By the end of the fall semester, she was down to 102 pounds. She was also chronically tired, had trouble concentrating, and occasionally fainted. Still, when Hillary looked in the mirror, she saw a fat, homely young woman who needed to lose more weight.[9]

Hillary's self-starvation was severe enough that she was diagnosed with anorexia nervosa, one of the three types of eating disorders recognized by psychologists and psychiatrists (the other two are bulimia nervosa and binge-eating disorder). Women with anorexia nervosa starve themselves until they are 15 percent or more below a normal body weight for their height, and still they feel fat. Their entire self-worth rests on being extremely thin.

In both bulimia nervosa and binge-eating disorder, women (again, the disorder afflicts mostly women) binge eat. In addition, in bulimia nervosa (but not in binge-eating disorder), women engage in purging behaviors to get rid of the food they just ate, or the weight they fear gaining. Purging is not pretty—vomiting is a favored method, along with laxative abuse. Some women also engage in extreme exercising in an attempt to purge their weight.

What constitutes a binge? A binge is technically defined as eating an amount of food that is larger than what most people would eat in a relatively short period of time, such as an hour or two.[10] The size of a binge can vary from woman to woman. The average binge is about 1,500 calories, but about a third of binges are only 600 calories and another third are over 2,000 calories. Some women consider eating just one piece of cake a binge. What binges have in common is the sense that control over eating has been lost, and that you feel compelled to eat even though you aren't hungry.

While most girls and women don't cross the line into an eating disorder, they do spend days and nights closely monitoring how much they eat, how much their friends are eating, and evaluating their self-worth based on the ability to control what goes into their mouth. In the study I mentioned earlier, I asked women to rate how important it was for them to look good to others versus how important it was for their body to be healthy and well. Forty percent of young adult women and 31 percent of the middle-aged women rated their looks as more important than their body's functioning.

You might think that women who care more about how their body looks than how healthy it is would be especially careful to watch what they eat. Ironically, women who scored higher on concern about their looks were more likely to binge eat when they were upset than women who were less concerned. It seems that women's tendency to cope with their emotions by doing something with their body, in this case binge eating, is so strong that even those who are excessively concerned with how they look turn to body-focused coping strategies when they are upset.

"I Don't Drink *That* Much"

Drinking-related problems in women have largely been ignored, in part at least, because we have been taught to expect men rather than women to suffer from them. True, men tend to drink more than women and are more likely to be diagnosed with alcoholism. But nationwide studies suggest that about 60 percent of women drink, and even more astounding, every month over 13 percent of women in America engage in heavy binge drinking (five or more drinks in a couple of hours). Statistics show, too, that 20 percent of women display some signs of alcohol abuse and 10 percent have drinking patterns so severe that they could be diagnosed with alcoholism at some point in their lives.

The image of an alcoholic in the popular mind is that of a binge drinker who goes on tears lasting days or weeks, consuming quarts of vodka, cases of beer, and magnums of wine all in a single evening. As troubling as these stories are, they are also comforting because they make our own drinking seem totally tame in comparison. "Whew! I'm clearly not an alcoholic—I've never come close to drinking that much!"

You may be shocked to learn that the latest dietary guidelines from the government suggest that a woman should never have more than one drink per day. "Oh well," you may say, "I don't drink every day so I can have more than one glass of wine when I do drink." But recent studies suggest that "heavy episodic drinking"—having three to four drinks a couple of nights per week—is more damaging to women's health than having a glass or two of wine each night.

How much can a woman drink before she is diagnosed as an "alcoholic"? In truth, the diagnosis of alcoholism has nothing to do with the quantity you drink. Instead, it depends on the consequences of alcohol use, at work, in social relationships, and to your physical health. Signs of alcohol-related disorders include frequently missing work or having trouble completing a project, friends and family expressing concern or harassing you about your drinking, and finally, drinking even after a physician suggests you should stop. Because the diagnostic criteria for alcoholism are subjective, it can be difficult to know when a person has crossed the line into a disorder, especially as girls and women may mask, or fail to share, just how troubled their lives have become. Consider, for example, fifty-seven-year-old Vicki, a full-time homemaker and mother of three.

Vicki's children, all of whom share her blond Nordic looks, are grown, in college or in jobs, with families and lives of their own. As a result, Vicki doesn't see them nearly as often as she'd like. Since her youngest child left home, she has felt lost and abandoned, unsure whether she has accomplished as much as she should have by this point in her life. Without motivation to go to work or try something new, Vicki just feels as if there is a tremendous weight on her that rarely lifts for more than an hour or two at a time.

Alcohol has always been part of Vicki's adult life—drinks before dinner, wine with dinner, and cocktail parties on the weekends at the country club. In the last few years, she's noticed that she gets intoxicated on much less alcohol than it used to take in her younger days. Vicki keeps telling herself she should cut back on her drinking. But when she and her husband, Tom, settle down for before-dinner drinks, she feels a little less lonely and depressed than she did earlier in the day, and so she continues to have a couple of drinks before dinner. Then Tom usually opens a bottle of wine to have with the meal. Now that they have enough money to buy good wine, Vicki hates to deprive herself, and typically drinks

her half of the bottle. By bedtime, she is tipsy enough to of-
ten fall asleep on the couch, where she finds herself when she
wakes up at 4 A.M. Many mornings she skips her exercise
class at the club, feeling she couldn't possibly drag her body
through the aerobics routine.

Vicki's sense of sadness, her lethargy, lack of motivation,
and problems sleeping have increased in recent months to the
point that she sometimes spends all day in bed. She thinks her
drinking may feed her symptoms of depression. But the little
bit of relief she gets each night when she drinks with Tom
makes it really hard for her to forgo alcohol altogether.

Vicki may not seem like a classic alcoholic—she doesn't drink vast amounts of alcohol at one time, she restricts her drinking to dinner with her husband, and she isn't out on the road careening around in a drunken stupor. But Vicki's symptoms could qualify for a diagnosis of alcohol dependence—the technical label for alcoholism. She repeatedly drinks more than she thinks she ought to, and although she tells herself she should cut down, she doesn't. Several mornings each week she has a hangover. Like many women, Vicki, as it turns out, has been following this pattern for many years, even though no one, including Vicki herself, has ever considered that she may be suffering from a serious psychiatric disorder.

The Tie That Binds

Although depression, unhealthy eating patterns, and heavy drinking can happen as individual problems, they more often happen in combination, because all three are tied to self-focused coping in women. These links first became evident in the community study I mentioned earlier in this chapter. We measured self-focused coping by asking if people coped with stressful events by "thinking about a recent situation, wishing it had gone better," "thinking about how upset I feel," "boiling inside, without showing it," and "keeping my feelings to myself." Both women and men who scored high on this measure of self-focused coping were more depressed and more likely to binge eat or turn to alcohol when they were upset. Women, overall, were significantly more prone to lapse into self-focused coping than men.

The links between self-focused coping and the toxic triangle are evident as early as adolescence. In a recent study of adolescent girls, my collaborators and I found that those who engaged in self-focused coping developed more symptoms of depression, bulimia, and substance abuse over a three-year period than those who didn't engage in self-focused coping.[11]

Just how does self-focused coping lead down the pathway to depression, unhealthy eating habits, and binge drinking? When you focus inward on all your concerns and how you feel about them, instead of taking action to overcome your problems, you start a chain reaction that can culminate in a disabling depression.[12] As you think about one major concern or problem in your life, you analyze it, wonder what it means for you, think about how overwhelmed you are, and possibly think you should do something in response to the problem. The more you think, however, the bigger the problem becomes, just like a snowball rolling down a hill. Then this problem reminds you of another problem in your life, which you begin analyzing as well. Thoughts of more problems join in, and pretty soon you have an avalanche of problems burying you. Even if you have generated a solution to your first problem, you now feel so overwhelmed by those that have taken its place that you can't take action. You just curl up in a little ball, crushed and suffocating under the weight of your concerns.

Some women try to eat their way out of this crush of negative feelings. Binge eating can serve as a temporary distraction from feelings of sadness and despair, or feelings of rage against others that you aren't allowed to express.[13] Psychologist Eric Stice of the University of Texas at Austin followed a group of adolescent girls for two years, looking for predictors of binge eating.[14] He found that girls who engaged in emotional eating—eating when they felt distressed in an attempt to feel better—were significantly more likely to develop chronic binge eating over the two years.

One of the most famous binge eaters (and purgers) in history was Diana, Princess of Wales. The public had known for several years that Diana's marriage to Prince Charles was in trouble. Diana shocked the royal family and the public when she openly discussed her bulimia nervosa in a 1995 BBC interview:

I had bulimia for a number of years. And that's like a secret disease. You inflict it upon yourself. . . . You fill your stomach up four or five times a day—some do it more—and it gives you a feeling of comfort. It's like having a pair of arms around you, but it's temporary. Then you're disgusted at the bloatedness of your stomach, and then you bring it all up again. And it's a repetitive pattern which is very destructive to yourself.

Although Diana's life was extraordinary by any standard, the development of her bulimia contains themes that are very common. She suffered symptoms of depression, but because she felt pressured never to show weakness, even to her immediate family, the bulimia became a release valve for her negative emotions, while further damaging her self-esteem and sense of control.

Binge eating to quell negative feelings is sometimes referred to as *self-medicating*. The eating temporarily takes your mind off your troubles and makes you feel good again. But, as with Diana, the consequences of bingeing—the bloated feeling, weight gain, and shame associated with loss of control—backfire to increase the negative feelings that began the binge. Later you'll binge again to gain some relief from those feelings, which is how a self-perpetuating cycle of bingeing and self-loathing sets in.

Women also use alcohol to self-medicate against negative feelings. The alcohol temporarily drowns out their frustrations and concerns, and gives them a bit of release from their tight control over their emotions. Unfortunately, using alcohol to self-medicate can lead to a pattern of heavy drinking and abuse of alcohol, as we see with Brenda:

Brenda was a short, waiflike woman of twenty-seven who had had dreams of going to law school after college. Her college grades weren't that good, however, and her parents couldn't afford the tuition for law school. So, after college, Brenda began working in a government office, mostly doing boring paperwork. After work each night, she'd go home to her apartment and immediately pour herself a drink. She usually drank wine but sometimes she'd make herself a pitcher of margaritas. Brenda had learned in college that drinking made her feel happier and helped her forget the stresses of course work and exams. Her friends at college had all been heavy drinkers, and together they typically went to parties three or four nights per week. This was probably one reason why Brenda's grades had not been that strong, but being with her friends and drinking felt energizing, whereas studying did not.

These days, Brenda found herself craving a drink by about three in the afternoon. It frightened her a bit when she realized how much she actually needed that drink as soon as she got home. But she didn't see any real solution to her predicament, and she didn't see any reason to sit around being miserable every night when a little bit of wine could so swiftly lift her spirits.

In my research I have found that alcohol use for women, much more so than for men, is part of a more general pattern in which they ruminate about their worries and concerns but do not take action to overcome them.[15] Instead, women use alcohol to escape those worries and concerns for a while. Over time, these women are at higher risk of developing symptoms of alcohol abuse, such as losing a job due to drinking, or having conflicts with family members and friends because of their drinking.

Alcohol may be an especially attractive medicine for women who have spent their lives holding in their feelings, trying to conform to social pressures to be self-controlled and upbeat. Alcohol loosens your inhibitions. Words that you've wanted to say for years but felt you couldn't just fly out of your mouth. You find courage you didn't know you had to confront the people who make you feel bad.

Of course, you may say things you regret later. You may be punished by family and friends for your behavior, or for your loss of control, either of which will just make you feel worse. But the alcohol and the loss of control feel so good in the moment that you indulge them. Over time, a pattern of alcohol abuse and addiction can set in that is very hard to break.

Entering the Toxic Triangle

Many women first enter the toxic triangle in late childhood or adolescence when they begin to feel they don't quite fit in or measure up. They're not as good as the other girls—not as pretty, or smart, or athletic. They certainly don't have the relationships with boys that they want. They live with these feelings for months, maybe even years, doing okay but not great in school, having some, but never enough, friends. Life just seems hard, and it lacks the spark that they see in the lives of other girls. They are sort of depressed, but not really, not enough for anyone to notice or do anything about it.

They don't know what to do about these feelings and the concerns and dissatisfactions that are behind them. They don't really feel there is anything they *can* do. But still they think about their feelings and disappointments all the time, mulling them over, wondering what they mean. They worry that these feelings will go on forever. They compare themselves with other girls and feel they are uniquely incapable of improving their lives.

Then they discover the pleasures of drinking, or eating too much or too little. They find that they can hold their alcohol and that it makes them feel really good. Or they find that they feel really superior and strong when they stick to a strict diet and get really skinny.

Around age fourteen, Teresa, a tall, thin, sandy blond-haired girl from the upper Midwest, began to question everything, especially her own self-worth. She would go for weeks at a time feeling little motivation or energy to do her schoolwork. If her mother, who also had bouts of depression, would let her get away with it, Teresa would skip school and stay home in bed all day. At school, her grades were dropping. She did have one friend, Amy, who Teresa described as a "rough" girl—Amy was prone to swearing in almost every sentence, liked to dress in punk-style clothes, and was known to race around town on a motorized dirt bike. Amy introduced Teresa to beer one night when they were supposed to be hanging out at the mall. Amy's parents were working, so the girls went to Amy's house and downed a six-pack of beer in the space of an hour. Teresa felt more free and lighthearted than she had in months. So the next time they were out together, Teresa asked Amy if she knew how to get some beer. "No problem!" said Amy, who led them to the apartment of an "older" friend of hers who, in turn, went down the block to purchase several six-packs of Budweiser for them.

Over the next year or so, Teresa's drinking escalated until she was getting drunk most nights of the week. She felt terrible during the day, but the alcohol freed her inhibitions and drowned out her self-loathing thoughts, so she kept drinking. As she began to gain weight from the calories in the alcohol, this gave her even more to hate about herself.

Teresa decided she had to lose some weight, but because she didn't want to give up the beer, she had to cut back on the amount of food she ate. Teresa would go all day long barely eating anything, then would drink heavily at night. She did lose some weight, but because she was drinking so many calories in beer, she didn't lose very much. In addition, sometimes at night while she was drinking she got so hungry she would binge on junk food that Amy always seemed to have around. Teresa resolved that if she could just keep from gaining any more weight, everything would be okay. By the time she graduated high school, a regular pattern had developed: her days were spent avoiding food and feeling hungover and guilty, longing for a drink; at night she would consume as much beer as she could get her hands on, and if her willpower broke, binge on the junk food at a party or a friend's house.

When a girl drinks too much in an attempt to quell feelings of unworthiness and dissatisfaction with life, as Teresa did, it is easy for others to get hung up on her heavy drinking instead of dealing with the root of the problem. Teresa's family would be very frightened to discover how much she drinks, and with the best intentions might focus their concerns exclusively on getting her to stop. If she stops drinking without addressing her low self-esteem and general unhappiness, though, she'll still find herself trapped. She may stop drinking but also begin to starve herself in an attempt to feel "totally in control."

Doing Permanent Damage

It would be misleading to think that women's heavy drinking or chaotic eating patterns *always* develop as a result of depression and feelings of unworthiness. For a substantial number of women, drinking or unhealthy eating comes first, and depression develops as a result of the effects of these behaviors on her body and life.[16]

Before she married Bruce, Nicole didn't drink that much— she might have had a couple of beers or some wine when she was out to dinner at a nice restaurant with friends. But her job as an elementary schoolteacher demanded a lot of energy and concentration, so she usually avoided alcohol just to be able to keep up with the kids.

Bruce, on the other hand, usually had something to drink every night. He is a big man—6 foot 8 inches and 200 pounds—so he could hold a lot of alcohol. Bruce fancied himself a wine expert, and he often took clients out for dinner at nice restaurants, where the maître d' would suggest an expensive bottle of wine to go with the meal. Because he was chief account manager for a brokerage firm, Bruce had a generous expense account and usually ordered at least two bottles of wine over the course of the evening for him and his guest.

Nicole was captivated by Bruce's sophistication, and when they were dating she tried to match him, drink for drink. She usually paid a price in energy and general well-being the next day—she was tired, grumpy, and had trouble concentrating—but she was so in love with Bruce that she didn't care and would drink just as much the next time they went out.

Once they were married, Nicole cut back somewhat on her drinking. But Bruce sometimes kidded her for being a prude and not being as fun a dinner partner as she had been when they were dating. Under pressure, Nicole would have "one more glass" (which usually led to two or three more glasses) of wine that evening. She did indeed

*feel that drinking helped smooth out conversations be-
tween her and Bruce, and this motivated her to put aside
her concerns about how she would feel the next day. Then
she'd toss and turn all night, her sleep disrupted by the alcohol, and wake up the next morning kicking herself for
feeling terrible again on a school day.*

*By the time Nicole and Bruce had been married a year,
Nicole was drinking nightly with Bruce, and they regularly
polished off a couple of bottles of wine each night. She began falling behind in her work, unable to get any lesson
plans or grading done in the evenings. She increasingly had
to call in sick for work because of hangovers—at first only
occasionally, and then more regularly, even weekly. The
students began reporting to their parents that Nicole was
irritable with them, and even fell asleep at her desk at times
while they were quietly working on their own. The princi-
pal of her school called Nicole in to confront her about her
behavior, warning that if it continued, he would not renew
her contract at the end of the year. Nicole was ashamed and
devastated that her promising career as a teacher seemed to
be in jeopardy.*

Heavy drinking or unhealthy eating patterns often develop in
an attempt to manage a relationship with a man. We want to impress a guy by keeping up with him drink for drink. But our
bodies are smaller and don't metabolize alcohol as well as men's
so we can't hold as much. Because we're more focused on manag-

ing our relationships than taking care of ourselves, we often don't notice how drunk we're getting, or how often we're getting drunk.

In the meantime, life gets more and more out of control. The toxic effects of alcohol on our brains make us tired, lethargic, and moody. Drinking can leave us to neglect other important aspects of our lives—our relationships with other women, moving forward in our career, our health—which can make us even more depressed, leading us to turn for solace wherever we can find it.

Even though Nicole's problems didn't begin with feelings of depression, they resulted from self-focused coping. Nicole tried to manage her relationship with Bruce by controlling her own body in an unhealthy way. She denied and ignored the signs her body was giving her that she was drinking too much, and tried to change how she reacted rather than changing her pattern of interaction with Bruce. Why was it so important to him that she continue to drink heavily with him? Why did they need alcohol to have "smooth" conversations together? These are questions Nicole avoided confronting, in favor of trying to cope by forcing her body to take in more alcohol than was healthy for her.

Escaping the Toxic Triangle

Effectively and permanently escaping the toxic triangle requires understanding how it affects women's lives and how it evolves. We must confront the danger the toxic triangle poses to our own lives, and the lives of our daughters, sisters, and women friends. By first recognizing the social, psychological, and biological forces that pull women into the toxic triangle, we can design strategies that capitalize on women's strengths to break free of these forces.

Just How Toxic the Triangle Is

THE TOXIC TRIANGLE of yo-yo eating, heavy drinking, and depressive symptoms reflects a complete breakdown of effective coping and the takeover of self-focused coping. Rather than doing something about the problems that are upsetting them, women who fall into the toxic triangle hold their concerns in their minds and their bodies. They ruminate on their troubles and concentrate on their bodies—focusing on how their bodies feel, trying to change those feelings, or attempting to control their bodies—rather than taking action to overcome the true sources of their distress.

Self-focused coping shuts out effective help from others. Family members and friends grow confused by the shifting picture of "the problem" that a woman presents—one day she's depressed, another day she's drinking, another day she's binge eating. They may try to help her with one problem, just to have another pop up. Family members become overwhelmed, frustrated, defeated, even pull away. If a woman consults a physician or therapist, he or she is also likely to focus only on one of her problems, likely her worst one, but ignore the others.

Jill, the account executive we met in chapter 1, was occasionally confronted by her family members about her behaviors. As is often the case, her family tended to focus on her eating habits and her drinking, because they were the most visible signs of the toxic triangle. Another reason family members focus on a woman's heavy drinking is because it carries a social stigma that can reflect on the family.

Jill's sister, Sarah, was the one who most often said something to her about her behaviors. "You drink too much," Sarah would say as the two of them were clearing away dishes after Sunday dinner with their parents, and Jill was sipping her third glass of wine that evening. "You're going to ruin your career and your health. And you need to eat more and stop worrying so much about being skinny."

Jill could easily blow off Sarah's comments. Jill's job provided much more money and prestige than Sarah's job as a part-time manager of a clothing store ever would. Sarah had always battled her weight and had been even more self-conscious about her shape than Jill was. So, rather than taking Sarah's comments seriously, Jill just ignored them as the product of sisterly envy and bossiness. Sometimes, if she was annoyed enough at Sarah, Jill accused her of jealousy. Most

*of the time, though, she just said, "Mind your own business,"
and diverted the subject to something else.*

Our Eyes Shut Tight

Because women take it upon themselves to manage stress by managing their thoughts and bodies, rather than taking out stress on
others, their suffering is easy to ignore. You can see this in the
amount of attention and money spent on the externalizing mental
health problems that males more often suffer—such as antisocial
behavior and attention deficit hyperactivity disorder—compared
to the self-focused mental health problems that females more often suffer. The externalizing disorders that men and boys suffer
wreak havoc on society in the form of property damage and violent attacks on others. In response, we spend millions of dollars
trying to treat men and boys and contain these behaviors.

Because the quieter problems of girls and women don't bother
other people nearly as much, they are not dealt with. Even when it
comes to alcohol abuse, women tend to be quiet. Compared to
men, many women are "gentle drinkers." When they are inebriated, women don't tend to become as loud and obnoxious as
men, if only because even inebriated women generally attempt to
project an aura of traditional "feminine" submissiveness (whereas men may feel freer to fulfill traditional "masculine" behaviors
of confrontation and bravado). Physicians don't regularly ask
women about their alcohol use, so don't get the opportunity to notice trouble. Friends of a woman who drinks too much are often

drinking heavily themselves, so they have no motivation to confront her about her drinking. The ease with which men's antisocial drunkenness is seen as a problem allows society to remain ignorant of women's less obvious, more "quiet" forms of drunkenness.

A factor leading us to ignore depression and eating disorders in women is the belief that this is "just how women are." We expect women to be moody or sullen, so when they are, we write it off as part of their character, or just a hormonal phase. No big deal, she'll snap out of it eventually, pay her no mind. If she talks constantly about her weight or what she's eaten, well, that's the way women are. If you're a guy, just ignore her. If you're a woman, you're likely to be similarly concerned about your weight, and fall easily into an intense conversation about carbs and fat grams and calorie burn.

In stark contrast, because we *don't* expect women to have alcohol problems, we remain oblivious to the problem's pervasiveness. A broad conspiracy of silence and denial surrounding women's drinking problems exists among friends, family members, and physicians.

As most of us now recognize, large corporations profit from women's preoccupations with their bodies. Women, more than men, spend billions of dollars every year on products and services to reduce their weight and control their eating, including expensive weight-loss programs, pills to curb appetite, health club memberships, and surgeries to remove fat.

The alcohol industry needs women. The overall rate of alcohol consumption has declined in recent decades, leaving the liquor and wine industries eager to promote drinking as a good thing for women. Advertisements depict women drinkers as sexy and young, having a great time, attracting handsome men. Savvy beverage industry executives have helped their companies make billions off wine coolers and spritzers specifically invented to be light and sweet enough to appeal to women. The same executives have made sure that the public is exposed to countless media stories about the health benefits of drinking. Of course, what we are not told is that many of those supposed benefits may only be true for men, and that even moderate levels of drinking raise a woman's risk of developing numerous deadly disorders and diseases.

When it comes to depression, the pharmaceutical companies are only too happy to trumpet the high rate of depression in women, who make up over two-thirds of the market for antidepressant drugs. These drugs have been lifesavers for many women, but they don't "cure" depression—they only keep the symptoms of depression at bay. Antidepressants don't address the social and psychological forces that push women into depression, disordered eating, and alcohol problems. They don't help us understand and confront women's tendency to cope with situations by self-focusing. They do allow us to respond to women who are trapped in the toxic triangle with the simple phrase "go take your pills."

These multibillion-dollar industries are not the single cause of the toxic triangle, but they help to create a culture of expectations for women and how they will relate to their bodies and minds. These expectations are like a drumbeat in the background—

after a while, you don't even consciously hear it, but you are nonetheless walking in step with the beat.

Documenting the Damage

It's not just family and friends who have ignored the toxic triangle in women. Clinicians and researchers focus on one component of the triangle at a time, rather than documenting the long-term effects on women's lives of combinations of depression, disordered eating, and heavy drinking.

Fortunately, this gap in the research is beginning to be filled. One critically important research project, run by psychologists Peter Lewinsohn, Paul Rohde, John Seeley, and Ruth Striegel-Moore, followed over a thousand young adolescents in the general community in Oregon over several years, reporting on the ebb and flow of symptoms of depression, eating disorders, and drinking problems. They found that those adolescents who had a combination of two or three of these problems were much more likely than those who had only one to have trouble in school, to fight with their parents, to attempt suicide, and generally to function poorly in many areas of their lives.[1] It seems that adolescents who fall into one branch of the toxic triangle can break free of it or contain its damage to some extent. In contrast, those who reach the place where two or three components of the triangle intersect can become immobilized, unable to do everyday schoolwork or to take comfort from friends. They may use extreme measures— even suicide attempts—to try to escape the toxic triangle.

Psychologist Eric Stice of the University of Texas at Austin has specifically focused on the combination of binge-eating behaviors and depressive symptoms, identifying two types of binge eating. One type, which I'll call the dieting type, is connected to excessive attempts at losing weight. Women with the dieting type are greatly concerned about their body shapes and sizes, and try their best to maintain a strict low-calorie diet, while frequently falling off the wagon and engaging in binge eating. These women often use vomiting or exercise to try to purge themselves of the food or the weight that bingeing puts on their bodies. In the other type of binge eating, the depressive type, women are equally concerned about their weight and body sizes but are also plagued by feelings of depression and low self-esteem, so they often eat to quell these feelings.

Stice and his colleagues have found that women with the depressive type of disordered eating pattern suffer even greater social and psychological consequences, over time, compared to women with the dieting type of disordered eating.[2] Depressive eaters have more difficulties in their relationships with family and friends, are more likely to suffer significant psychiatric disorders such as anxiety disorders, and are less likely to respond well to treatment. One long-term study found that over a period of five years, women with the depressive type of eating problems were more likely to be diagnosed with major depression or an anxiety disorder, and were more likely to continue to engage in severe binge eating, compared to women who had the dietary type.[3] Indeed, 80 percent of the women with the depressive type developed full-blown major depression over those five years. The

lesson found here is that the intersection of depression and unhealthy eating patterns is more toxic for women than either of
these problems alone. When heavy drinking is added to the mix,
the combination is even more poisonous.

You Don't Need a Diagnosis to Suffer

Recent research also reveals that the devastating effects of the
toxic triangle do not come only to those women whose symptoms of depression, drinking, and unhealthy eating are severe
enough to qualify for a psychiatric diagnosis. Problems in each
of these three domains fall along a continuum, and even women
who suffer only moderate symptoms can incur major damage
to their health and well-being. Also, over time, moderate symptoms of depression, heavy drinking, and disordered eating tend
to evolve into more severe symptoms, dragging women deeper
and deeper into the triangle.

In the studies of adolescents in Oregon described earlier, researchers focused on what are called *partial-syndrome eating
disorders*—behaviors that smack of anorexia or bulimia nervosa
but don't meet the full criteria for the diagnoses.[4] Adolescents
with partial-syndrome eating disorders may binge at least once a
week, but not multiple times per week. They may be underweight,
but not a full 15 percent underweight. They tend to be highly
concerned with their weight and judge themselves on the basis of
it. Nonetheless, their symptoms don't add up to a full-blown eating disorder, just a partial one.

Adolescents with partial-syndrome eating disorders, the vast majority of whom were girls, were just as likely as those with full-blown eating disorders to experience multiple psychological problems, including anxiety disorders, substance abuse, depression, and attempted suicide, both as adolescents and in their twenties. In fact, almost 90 percent had a full-blown psychiatric disorder when they were in their early twenties. Those with partial-syndrome eating disorders also reported lower self-esteem, poorer social relationships, poorer physical health, and lower life satisfaction than those with no signs of an eating disorder. In addition, they were less likely to have earned a bachelor's degree, and more likely to be unemployed. Jenny is a young woman with a partial-syndrome eating disorder, which is ruining her enjoyment of life as a new mother.

When she was pregnant with her first child at the age of twenty-four, Jenny put on 50 pounds. She felt like a beach ball, as big around as she was tall, even after the baby was born. Jenny had always had a sweet tooth, and if she got a box of chocolates or other sweets for a present, she was known to eat the entire box in one sitting. While she was pregnant, her food cravings were out of control. One day she ate half of a carrot cake. Another day she had a Big Mac and supersize fries for lunch, then an hour later had a Whopper and an ice-cream sundae for dessert. In the two years since the baby was born, her binge eating has slowed down only a little. While the baby is sleeping, she might eat a whole can of Pringles, or all of the leftover casserole from last night's supper. Occasionally, Jenny will feel so disgusted with herself after bingeing that she'll go into the bathroom and try to throw it all up. She's successful only some of the time. A lot of the time, she just gags a lot and gives up, feeling even more ashamed and stupid.

Jenny is so embarrassed by her eating behaviors and her excess weight that she hasn't wanted to go out in public much. She and the baby have been invited to play groups, but she has made excuses not to go. Jenny had a good career as an accountant before she stopped working during the pregnancy. She always intended to go back to work once the baby was toddling. But now she can't imagine, with the way she looks, facing her old friends and the schoolchildren. She also has visions of getting caught bingeing in the employees' lounge. Jenny feels she's a failure, even though she is a great mother with a beautiful, healthy child.

Toxic to Our Relationships

The social isolation that Jenny is experiencing is greater than that of other young mothers, which is, unfortunately, common among women who are locked in the toxic triangle. You're ashamed and embarrassed. Just having a conversation with another person can seem like a monumental task. You may not even answer the phone or e-mails, because you just don't know what you would say to those who are trying to reach you.

It's not that women in the toxic triangle don't want others' support. In fact, they are often desperate for the love and under-standing of family members and friends but, like Jenny, don't know how to reach out for support. They become withdrawn, avoiding friends and family and turning down invitations for social outings. Symptoms of depression, or the fear that others disapprove of their eating or drinking habits, lead women em-broiled in the toxic triangle to reject others' overtures, preferring isolation to being intruded upon or controlled.

When they do connect, family members and friends don't al-ways respond effectively. While often intending to be supportive and understanding, they may not understand why a woman can't "pull herself up by the bootstraps" and "snap out of it." Frus-trated at their own ineffective nagging, they pull away, or con-tinue until she blows up at them.

Psychologist Thomas Joiner of Florida State University has identified a phenomenon that appears to contribute to some of the hostility and rejection that women in the toxic triangle expe-rience in their relationships: *excessive reassurance seeking*. Women who constantly ask family members and friends for assurance that they are loved and that they are good people are engaging in this phenomenon. Never satisfied with the assurances they get, instead they pester others to the point of driving them away. Rachel, a forty-eight-year-old homemaker from the Bronx, of-ten engages in excessive reassurance seeking in her interactions with her husband, Phil.

Phil never really gave Rachel good cause to doubt that he loved her. He was attentive and loving. He had been at her side when she had medical problems a few years ago, and when her mother died last year. He supported her decision to stay home to raise their two children, and was sincerely interested in what she and the kids did during the day while he was working at his law firm.

But still Rachel doubted, and these doubts had grown stronger in the last few months as another one of her depressive periods set in. How could he love her, when she was so boring? Surely he was just being nice when he asked about her day—he couldn't really be interested, given how exciting his own work was. She had gained weight over the years and felt she was no longer attractive to him. She wondered what he would do if one of the young women lawyers in his firm expressed interest in him.

Rachel tried to keep these concerns to herself, but they leaked out, in little comments to Phil. When he came home in the evening and said, "How was your day?" she sometimes responded, "Oh, boring as usual, you wouldn't be interested." Then she would wait to see what his response was. Phil would usually say something like, "Sure I'm interested, tell me what you did." Then Rachel would tell him a few incidents from the day, but label each one as "nothing" and "silly" as she went along. She listened intently for his response, wanting him to deny that her activities were nothing or silly, and becoming anxious and disappointed if he didn't explicitly do so.

When Rachel mentioned that she felt fat or unattractive, Phil would usually respond that she was still his beautiful *bride. She responded, "Oh, you have to say that, you're stuck with me." Phil felt frustrated and put off by this, but tried to stay calm. "I don't have to say that, I mean it. I love you, and I love how you look." But Rachel would not be satisfied: "You love me now, but will you always love me no matter what happens?"*

Rachel set up all sorts of other tests of Phil's love for her, and ploys to gain assurance of his devotion. If they disagreed with each other about something in the morning, Rachel would ruminate about it after Phil left for work. In her mind, she implicitly believed that if he hadn't called to talk with her about the disagreement by 10 A.M., this meant he was really angry and their relationship was in trouble. Sometimes, if he hadn't called or e-mailed her by 11 A.M., she'd call or e-mail him with a neutral message, just to see whether he'd mention that morning's disagreement. If he didn't respond almost immediately, Rachel took this as further evidence that he was angry with her, even though she knew he was probably just very busy. If he did respond to her message, but didn't mention the disagreement and how sorry he was for it, Rachel would ruminate about this for the rest of the afternoon. By the time Phil got home in the evening, she was ripe with fear and anger, while he hadn't thought about the disagreement all day because it had been so minor.

Excessive reassurance seeking and its opposite, self-isolation, are only two ways that women caught in the toxic triangle suffer damage to their close relationships. At the same time that women who seek assurance can be obsequious and deferential in an attempt to hold on to others, they can also be hostile and irritable as a reaction to the resentment they feel at their dependence. This resentment leaks out in small and large ways—snide remarks, snapping back unnecessarily, seeing ill will when none is meant. Interactions with spouses, family, and friends may be peppered with conflict and misunderstanding. They may even feel they have no influence over their children, or that their children do not love or respect them.

The toxic triangle can also erode intimacy by ruining women's sex lives. Even moderate amounts of alcohol can make it difficult for women to become fully aroused or have an orgasm. Women who drink heavily can experience difficulty becoming aroused even when they are fully sober. Depression also kills sexual arousal and desire. You're just not interested in sex anymore, and when you do have sex, you don't enjoy it as much. And if you take antidepressants to try to overcome the depression, one of the major side effects may rob you of your sexual desire and arousal.

Women who end up in the toxic triangle seem to be magnets for interpersonal stress.[5] They are more likely to marry men with psychological problems, including alcohol and drug problems and personality disorders, and they are then more likely to endure separations and divorces from their spouses. Their children are more likely to have problems in school or in their relationships with other children. Their friendships tend to be with those who have psychological problems, including depression, alcohol abuse, and eating disorders, only compounding the difficulty of escaping the toxic triangle. Indeed, these friendships may reinforce each woman's unhealthy behaviors.

This is how a self-perpetuating cycle gets set up. Women who are vulnerable to the toxic triangle often find themselves locked in highly stressful family environments that include conflict in their marriages, husbands who have serious psychological problems, and children who are troubled. These stressors make them feel more depressed and out of control, which only feeds their symptoms. The symptoms themselves can create more stressors by worsening conflict with others and making it even harder to function as mothers, partners, and friends to others.

When Toxic Becomes Deadly

The conflict that arises from a life lived inside the toxic triangle can be much more severe than ordinary marital or parental discord. Particularly for women who are drinking heavily, the conflict that arises can become violent and dangerous. One large study of 1,160 women found that over half of the serious sexual assaults experienced by women involved alcohol; in almost all these cases, the man who perpetrated the assault had been drinking; in the majority of cases, both the man and the woman had been drinking.[6] When husbands drink, or husbands and wives drink together, they are more likely to get into arguments, and even physical fights.[7]

We tend to think of alcohol-related violence as happening to poor, uneducated women who live in desperate areas. The reality is that much of the violence connected to alcohol happens to middle-class or upper-class women living in lovely homes with their seemingly nice families. Alcohol's unique ability to unleash simmering problems between a woman and her husband or partner often escalates, with him getting rough and her fighting back. Unfortunately, she's much more likely to get hurt than he is.

This was the pattern of interaction between Sandy and Bill, forty-year-old Polish-Americans living in New York. Their marriage had been in trouble for years. Most of their fights were over finances—Bill thought Sandy spent too much money on clothes, and she thought his endless "improvements" to the house were unnecessary expenses. They also fought about their two teenage children, who, they feared, were experimenting with drugs as well as alcohol. These fights were usually just loud shouting matches that ended with one or both of them retreating to the bedroom and slamming the door. Often, though, these fights would erupt after Sandy and Bill had had quite a bit to drink. When she was sober, Sandy tried to watch what she said during a fight so as not to immediately "push Bill's buttons" and send him into a rage. When she drank too much, however, Sandy went right for those buttons and pushed as hard as she could. Most of the time, Bill would stomp off in a rage, jumping into his car and careening down the street, to be gone the rest of the night.

Occasionally, a shoving match would emerge during one of these fights. Sometimes it wasn't really clear who started the physical contact between them, but it was always clear that Sandy got the rougher treatment. Bill was 50 pounds heavier so his shoves could send Sandy, who was only 5 foot 3 and 120 pounds, hurling across the floor. She might get right up and start punching on him, but he could pin her arms behind her back with little effort. More than once, Sandy woke up the next morning after one of these fights with bruises and cuts. About a month ago, on a rainy Friday night, she broke her arm in a hard landing after one of Bill's rough shoves that this time sent her tumbling down a flight of stairs.

Why do violence and alcohol go together? Alcohol increases physiological arousal, and men are more likely than women to act on this through aggression, sometimes toward their women partners. Research also shows that men, more than women, tend to associate alcohol consumption with feelings of dominance and power. Intoxicated men may be more likely to see women who have been drinking as more vulnerable to domination or more socially deviant and therefore deserving of punishment. Intoxicated women, in turn, appear more likely to retaliate violently when attacked by their intoxicated male partners, leading to an escalation of violence. Perhaps not surprisingly, in most cases the woman is much more likely than the man to suffer significant harm in these encounters.

Toxic to Our Careers

The interpersonal effects of the toxic triangle are not restricted to women's personal lives. Being withdrawn and socially isolated, and being irritable and excessively seeking reassurance, are behaviors that can wreak havoc on our careers.

Other symptoms of the toxic triangle make it very hard to perform well at work. It's difficult to concentrate if you're depressed, hungover, or preoccupied with food, and so you may read the same page of a report over and over but still not know what it said. Your memory may fail you, leading you to forget both small and important things. Making decisions seems impossible, so you may remain immobilized at the worst possible moment, when the situation calls for decisive action. As a result, you may have difficulty keeping up with your work, and the work that you do may suffer in quality.

One recent nationwide study focusing specifically on depression found that over half of depressed people said their work was moderately or severely affected by their depressive symptoms.[8] On average, people with depression experienced 35 days of the previous year in which they were totally unable to work or carry out their normal activities. The other two components of the toxic triangle can effect their own damage. Women with eating disorders or drinking problems are more likely than women without these problems to be unemployed or underemployed. When the three branches of the toxic triangle join together, it can stop a career dead in its tracks, as was nearly the case with Catherine.

At the age of forty-three, Catherine was considered a successful businesswoman by most people who knew her. She had opened her shop on a busy street in Chicago eleven years ago, and after a rocky start, it had been thriving for the last few years. Catherine imported beautiful hand-embroidered clothes from Latin America, and the intricate and colorful designs on the clothes were a big hit. Catherine always wore one of the blouses or dresses from her collection when she was in the store, and her dark features and tall, slender body showed off the clothes stunningly.

For the last year, however, Catherine has had difficulty keeping up with her business. After a messy divorce from her husband, she felt drained of all energy. Most nights, she was up half the night, worrying about work, wondering how her marriage had gone so wrong, and questioning what her life meant. She would often binge eat when she had insomnia, and had gained 35 pounds. She could no longer fit into many of the blouses she had brought home from her store.

When Catherine went on her usual buying trip to Latin America in January, she had great difficulty deciding what she should buy. Several times she found herself standing in front of a collection of clothes, supposedly choosing those she would buy, immobilized with doubt and indecision. She returned to Chicago with half the number of items she usually bought, far less than she needed going into the summer season.

Back in Chicago, Catherine began to receive phone calls from her creditors asking for payments. Usually a prompt and reliable bill-payer, Catherine had completely forgotten about some bills and had actually lost others. Her good credit rating with her vendors and her bank was in jeopardy.

At the shop, Catherine often felt irritable and impatient with her employees. They seemed so uninterested in their work, and she suspected some of them of stealing merchandise. The truth was that Catherine's negative and hostile demeanor had put a black cloud over everyone in the shop, bringing their own moods down and making everyone more grumpy. Catherine had lost a couple of her best employees in the last year, after she had snapped their heads off for nothing or indirectly accused them of cheating her.

Catherine had built a brilliant business based on her keen eye for fashion and her retail savvy. Her symptoms of depression—the problems concentrating and making decisions, the irritability, the immobilization—although understandable following her divorce, were jeopardizing all she had built for herself. Rather than acknowledging she needed help, Catherine turned to binge eating for short-term solace. Her weight gain only added to her problems, giving her more to worry about and hate herself for.

Toxic to Our Health

Even if we could shield our relationships from the effects of the toxic triangle and keep trudging along in our careers despite our symptoms, our physical health can suffer. We have lots of information about what each of the three components of the toxic triangle does to our health—when two or three of these problems are present in a woman's life, her physical health may be tragically damaged.

ONE DRINK TOO MANY

Thousands of women across the nation are unknowingly drinking themselves into early graves. Because women's bodies do not metabolize alcohol as efficiently as men's, and because women are simply smaller on average than men, alcohol has a more noxious effect on all key organ systems—including the heart, liver, and brain.[9] Even mild levels of daily drinking—for instance, consuming just two or three glasses of white wine per night—may seriously increase women's risk for breast cancer, and may lead to a number of reproductive health problems (such as infertility).[10] More serious levels of drinking can literally eat a woman's insides.

We've all heard in the media about the cardiac benefits from moderate drinking, and many women and men who have a drink or two per day do so thinking it makes for a healthy heart. What we don't hear in the media is that the cardiac benefits of alcohol don't apply to women, at least to young and middle-aged women. On the other hand, consuming as little as two drinks per day can begin to inflict serious harm on women's hearts.[11] Perhaps most frightening, the overall rate of alcohol-related mortality among heavy drinkers in our nation today is four times greater for women than for men. When it comes to alcohol-related deaths in America, every year we're burying four times more heavy-drinking women than men.

Research shows, too, that alcohol more seriously affects women's overall ability to function than it does men's.[12] After just a drink or two, many women begin to have trouble walking straight and thinking straight. As a result, women are more likely than men to be involved in car crashes and other accidents after drinking.

Lucy is a woman who, thankfully, became aware of the toxic effects alcohol was having on her body.

Lucy is a thirty-year-old single woman from Phoenix who works as a real estate agent. Her dark pretty features— beautiful brown eyes and long black hair—do nothing to mitigate her feelings of unattractiveness because she is 20 pounds overweight. She believes her weight is the main reason she doesn't have a steady male friend. Lucy works hard at having a social life, going out for dinner most nights with friends and to parties most weekends. She's one of those women who can hold her alcohol—or at least thinks she can—and so tends to have at least three glasses of wine many nights each week.

A few months ago, Lucy began to have dizzy spells for no apparent reason. Since she has almost always been on a diet, she attributed them to hunger. Even more worrisome was the increasing blurriness in her vision and her need to pee all the time. When she mentioned these symptoms to her physician, he ordered a fasting blood test, which suggested Lucy had developed moderate diabetes. Lucy thought this was absurd, given that she had no family history of diabetes and was so young. Nonetheless, the doctor gave her a diet to follow, and strongly recommended she stop drinking.

Lucy decided to follow the diet, which seemed like a good one for losing some weight, but refused to stop drinking. Her glasses of wine were too much a part of her social life, and she desperately worried that men would find her even less attractive if she was a teetotaler. In spite of the force of her denial, Lucy's symptoms of diabetes were getting worse, and she even began to have severe dizzy spells while driving.

Lucy was fortunate that on a subsequent visit to her physician he stressed the toxic effects that alcohol was having on her body. She began to work with a psychologist who helped her feel better about her body and her life, which in turn gave her the emotional support she needed to stop drinking. Of course, as lucky as Lucy was to get the information and support she needed, many, if not most, women who develop alcohol-related diseases may never realize the harm they're inflicting on their organs with every sip they take. Tragically, many women only realize what they're doing when it's too late.

DANGER: FOOD!

Whether you eat too much or too little, your physical health can be strongly affected by crazy eating patterns. Binge eating is strongly linked to obesity, and obesity can lead to diabetes, stroke, heart attacks, and other debilitating conditions. It's estimated that health problems caused by obesity now cost the health care system $117 billion per year.

On the opposite end of the spectrum, women who starve themselves also endanger their physical health. Prolonged starvation can lead to cardiovascular disease and heart failure, metabolic dysfunctions, dehydration, anemia, and susceptibility to bleeding, hypothermia, and a number of gastrointenstinal complications, including acute expansion of the stomach. The damage anorexia does to the immune system may make some anorectic women more vulnerable to severe illness.[13]

Although the death rate among women with bulimia nervosa is not as high as among those with anorexia nervosa, bulimia still has serious medical complications. One of the most deadly is an imbalance in the body's electrolytes, which results from fluid loss following excessive and chronic vomiting, laxative abuse, and diuretic abuse. Electrolytes are biochemicals that help regulate the heart, and imbalances in electrolytes can lead to heart failure.

DEPRESSED HEALTH

It's a little less obvious how depression affects physical health, but it does. For reasons we do not yet totally understand, people who are moderately to severely depressed have more illnesses than people who never get depressed.[14] The range of illnesses includes colds, the flu, and also more severe illnesses, such as cardiovascular disease, stroke, and multiple sclerosis. For example, depressed people are significantly more likely to have complications following heart surgery or even multiple heart attacks. Likewise, liver disease, so often caused by alcohol abuse, does not respond as well to treatment in depressed patients.

It Never Seems to End

One reason the toxic triangle takes such a toll on physical health, careers, and interpersonal relationships is that the three health problems associated with the triangle tend to be chronic, lasting at least months and usually years. One study of 431 people with major depression that followed them an average of nine years found they had moderate to severe symptoms of depression 59 percent of the time and were symptom-free only 27 percent of the time.[15] Alcohol abuse, anorexia, bulimia, and binge-eating disorder also tend to be chronic conditions. Long-term studies show that although symptoms of the disorders may wax and wane, over half of women with one of these disorders continue to have symptoms for at least five to ten years.[16] Even if a woman escapes the toxic triangle free and clear for a time, she remains at high risk for relapse.

Women in the toxic triangle continue to have symptoms chronically, in part, because the majority of them never seek care, or wait for years after their symptoms have begun to do so.[17] Often this is because they don't have the money or insurance to pay for care, or because they are ashamed of their symptoms and don't want anyone to know about them. Other women believe they should be able to get out of the toxic triangle on their own because the symptoms are just a phase that will pass with time and won't affect their lives in the long run. This line of reasoning may be even more prevalent among women with moderate symptoms who often can keep going, dragging themselves through the day, never getting so impaired that friends or family push them into treatment.

Even as the more acute symptoms of the toxic triangle subside, some women seem to be left with lasting scars. Patterns of thought, self-image, social relationships, and academic and work lives are changed for the worse and can remain impaired for long periods after the symptoms have passed. Even if they don't relapse into new episodes, women with previous episodes of depression, disordered eating, and/or heavy drinking tend to have other enduring problems. Their functioning on the job may remain below par. They're not as interested in sex or don't enjoy it as much as they did before they fell into the triangle. And persisting through this is a chronic conflict and dissatisfaction with their friends and families.[18]

The toxic triangle may be most likely to leave psychological and social scars if a woman initially finds herself there during adolescence, rather than during adulthood.[19] A person's sense of self—who she is and what she believes—is still being developed in adolescence, much more than it is in adulthood. Depression or obsession with how you look can retard the development of your sense of self, creating long-lasting effects. During adolescence, skills and abilities accumulate; symptoms that interfere with memory, attention, and learning, such as the symptoms of the toxic triangle, can damage adolescents' achievement for the long term. Finally, adolescents are dependent on and connected with other people to a greater extent than are adults, so the hostility and irritability that goes hand in hand with the toxic triangle can significantly harm the social skills on which personal relationships depend.

Escaping from the toxic triangle requires that we first understand the journey into it—the social, psychological, and biological forces that pull us into this vortex and keep us trapped there. Only when we begin to see these forces at work in our own lives can we design strategies to bypass or conquer them and regain control over our health.

THREE

▼

A Woman's Place

We EXPECT DIFFERENT things of women and men, from their different roles in everyday life, to the behaviors that are deemed acceptable for one gender but not the other. Although social pressures for women and men to conform to traditional gender roles have eased a bit in recent decades, they still exist, exerting a heavy influence on our reactions to each other and the expectations we have for ourselves. Women's tendencies to engage in self-focused coping and then fall into the toxic triangle of depression, disordered eating, and heavy drinking are the consequences, at least in part, of adherence to gender roles.

No Other Choice

From a very young age, girls are molded and pressured into self-focused coping.[1] When a little girl is confronted with an upsetting situation, her parents often ask her about how she feels, sympathize with her feelings of distress, or encourage her to talk at length about the situation. What they don't do, at least not as much as they do with little boys, is help the girl move from an exploration of her feelings into doing something to change the situation. Parents are in general less likely to encourage in girls an action-oriented, problem-solving approach to dealing with difficult situations than they are with boys.

Now I acknowledge that parents may sometimes not do enough to encourage expression of emotions in their sons. Harvard psychologist William Pollock, in his book *Real Boys, Real Men,* argues that because parents discourage emotion in their boys, boys lose the ability to articulate and understand their emotions. Pollock also argues that the "big boys don't cry" message that parents often send their boys fosters the development of aggression and other acting-out behaviors in boys. Not only are boys not encouraged to express negative emotions, they are directly punished for doing so by disapproving parents, teachers, and other children. So they learn to ignore or shut out what they can't reveal, but these emotions burst out nonetheless as aggressive and harmful acts toward others.

When it comes to girls, the pendulum often swings too far the other way. It's as if the message girls get is "Big girls DO cry.

And cry, and cry, and cry." As a result, girls don't learn as many strategies for moving from being upset to doing something about it. They don't learn how to soothe their own negative feelings and turn their attention to possible solutions; instead they remain mired in feelings of distress and increasingly overwhelmed and immobilized. Or they take control over the only thing they can control—their body—and try to change how they feel with food or drink.

Consider this interchange between six-year-old Kristin and her mother, Susan, after Kristin has had an argument with a friend of hers at school:

> Susan: What's the matter, sweetie, why are you crying?
>
> Kristin: Jennifer told me she hates me!
>
> S: Why would she say something like that?
>
> K: I don't know. She's just being mean!
>
> S: No, I'm sure she has some reason. This is really upsetting you, isn't it?
>
> K: Yeah. (sniffles and tears)
>
> S: Mommy understands. I get really upset when other people are angry with me also. It makes me feel like crying and locking myself in my room.
>
> K: Yeah.
>
> S: What are you feeling right now, honey?
>
> K: Mad.
>
> S: Mad? But if you're crying, you must also be feeling sad. Do you feel sad, honey?
>
> K: Yeah.

S: I had a friend get angry with me the other day—you know
   her, Mrs. Murdo—and I came home and really felt like
   crying and wanting just to curl up in a little ball.

Susan's intentions in encouraging Kristin to talk at length
about her feelings and worries are good. In fact, that is what
many parenting books say you're supposed to do. And that's
what little girls want to talk about, right? While the kind of
mirroring Susan is doing here, using examples from her own life
to show that she understands how Kristin feels, can be an effective way of validating another person's feelings, it can also send
some pretty damaging, unintended messages. Susan not only lets
Kristin know she's faced similar situations, she makes it clear to
Kristin that she, too, finds such situations overwhelming. The
mother articulates her own concerns about conflicts with others
but doesn't go on to explain how she has handled these concerns
in the past, except to become upset. The message Kristin may take
from this interchange is that even Mom finds such situations impossible to deal with, so how could she, Kristin, possibly deal
with them except to become upset?

When a mother is herself depressed, she is especially likely to
draw her daughter into conversations about her own feelings and
even her sense of incompetence at handling daily life. Researcher
Hyman Hops and his colleagues at the Oregon Research Institute
observed interactions between mothers and their daughters and
found that depressed mothers were more likely than nonde-
pressed mothers to talk with their daughters about negative feelings and negative interpretations of recent events.[2] Depressed

mothers are, however, less likely to draw their sons into such conversations. Hops suggests that the daughters of depressed mothers become sounding boards for their mothers' feelings of sadness, anxiety, and self-loathing.

Anger: Don't Go There

There are male emotions and there are female emotions—at least there are emotions that are okay for males to experience and express and emotions that are okay for females to experience and express. Boys and men can be angry, but they can't be sad or afraid. Girls and women can be sad or afraid, but they can't be angry.

It's not that girls don't feel anger as much as boys—many studies of children and adults have shown that females are just as likely as males to become angry when they are cheated, insulted, or transgressed in some way. It's that girls, and women, are not allowed to express this anger, and as a result learn to squash it and hold it in.[3]

A few years ago, I did a combination of studies with two graduate students, Lisa Butler and Cheryl Rusting, that showed how differently women handle feelings of anger and sadness. In one study, we asked women undergraduates to come into our lab and spend a few minutes reading a story about an anger-provoking situation (being cheated out of a grade by a teaching assistant).[4] We then asked them to imagine themselves in that situation. Our intent was to coax these women into an angry mood for a short while, and when we asked them how they felt after imagining themselves in the situation, we found that they did indeed feel angry. We then gave them the option of writing one of two short essays: an essay about their typical emotional experiences or an essay describing their dormitory or living room. We were interested in whether the women, when they were in an angry mood, would choose to write about (or focus on) their emotions, or would choose not to focus on their emotions in this way. Seventy percent of the women chose *not* to write about their emotions, preferring to write about their dorm or living room.

When it comes to feelings of sadness, women make different choices. In a second study, we asked women to imagine themselves in a very sad situation.[5] Then we gave them the option of continuing to think about how they were feeling, or moving on to a boring geography task. In this case, the women overwhelmingly chose to continue thinking about their sad feelings, rather than complete the distracting geography task. This combination of data showed that when it comes to angry feelings, women don't want to go there, but when it comes to sadness, they are ready to dwell on these feelings.

It's not just parents who socialize girls and boys into "gender appropriate" expressions of emotion. Teachers reward girls more than boys for compliant, dependent behavior—for being good little girls. And children themselves enforce our cultural norms of how girls should act. An assertive, in-your-face little girl is a pariah among other girls, just as a sensitive, more emotional little boy is cruelly harassed by the other boys.

With all this pressure girls receive to suppress feelings of anger and frustration, but to experience feelings of sadness and anxiety, it's no wonder that they develop self-focused styles of coping. When they are upset, they are told to explore and articulate their negative feelings, as long as the feelings are directed at themselves and not at others. Sadness and anxiety are okay, even expected, in girls. So they nurture these feelings, expanding and growing them, and eventually may turn to binge eating and drinking to dull the pain the feelings cause. Anger, being not okay, requires that a lid be put on it; in worse cases, anger is transformed into self-doubt, or unhealthy behaviors such as yo-yo eating or heavy drinking.

Relationship Keepers

From a very early age, women are the keepers of relationships, responsible for everyone else's happiness, and for soothing bad feelings. Men rely on women to fulfill this role, and in close male-female relationships, women do the vast majority of the emotional work. Women draw men out to talk about how they feel, listen nonjudgmentally, console, encourage, and support them. When a relationship ends through breakup, divorce, or death, men usually seek a relationship with another woman to fill this gap in their lives.

How do girls learn to be the keepers of relationships? Again, they are taught, directly and indirectly, by adults. Psychologist Carolyn Zahn-Waxler has found that parents are much more likely to encourage girls than boys to empathize with other people. Parents point out to girls how others feel about situations, and make it clear that others' feelings are a major factor in how a girl should act. Parents are more likely to emphasize the harmful consequences to other people that would result from a girl expressing anger or, heaven forbid, retaliating against another person.

Partly as a result of this encouragement, girls recognize others' feelings and are acutely attuned to them. They take into consideration points of view other than their own and take other people's feelings into account when making their own decisions. As adults, women continue to be more sensitive toward others than men.

Women are also much more likely to define themselves in terms of their relationships with others—to think of themselves primarily as "the wife of . . ." or "the mother of . . ." Women's strong and close ties with friends and family are a major source of support in times of need. Indeed, women are much more likely than men to have a strong emotional support network come to their aid after a loss or a tragedy in their lives.

Unfortunately, some women cross a line into an excessive concern with the status of their relationships with others. Their only source of self-esteem is being "the wife of" or "the mother of." Their own moods are unduly influenced by the moods of others. If her husband wakes up happy, she is happy, but if he wakes up grumpy, she remains fearful and sad. If her child had a good day at school, then she has had a good day.

Women who are excessively concerned with relationships also tend to let their opinions of themselves be unduly influenced by how they perceive others see them. In a study conducted by myself and psychologist Tomi-Ann Roberts, who is now at Colorado College, we gave women and men some challenging puzzle tasks to do. Then we gave half the women and half the men positive feedback about how they did on the tasks. The other half were given negative feedback. In truth, the feedback in both cases was bogus—not at all reflective of how the men or women actually did but randomly assigned. We then asked all participants how they thought they did on the puzzles. We found that the men thought they did well, regardless of what we told them about their performance. On the other hand, the women felt good about their performance if we told them they did well, but felt bad if we told them they had done poorly.

This was the typical style of Emily, a secretary for a construction firm:

Emily always tried to do her best at her job. Working at a construction firm was tough at times—she was the only woman in the business, and the guys could get pretty rough with their talk. Her boss, Mr. Maxwell, was a gruff old guy who tried to be nice and praise his workers, but often lapsed into yelling when he got frustrated with someone. Emily took every word he said to heart. One day she overheard Mr. Maxwell saying to a customer that since she had started working for him, Emily had cleaned up his accounting system so that he was collecting payments due much more efficiently and as a result showing a much better growth in his business. For the rest of that day, Emily felt like a queen. Another day, though, Mr. Maxwell barked at Emily for writing down an order from a customer incorrectly, and for the next week Emily felt ashamed and lived in fear of being fired.

Emily was also hypersensitive to what the construction workers said to her as they came in and went from the office. They weren't known for their political correctness, and sometimes would comment on her sexy blouse or whether she looked especially thin that day. On days when they said something that could be taken as a compliment, she felt good about how she looked. On days when they said nothing, she wondered if it was because they actually thought she looked unattractive, and that is how she felt about herself.

Psychologist Vicki Helgeson at Carnegie Mellon University has come up with a complicated name for crossing the line into an obsession with your relationships with others. She calls this *unmitigated communion,* meaning that an individual's close personal relationships are not tempered by an appropriate amount of concern for her own well-being. Helgeson's measure of unmitigated communion includes items such as "I always place the needs of others above my own." "For me to be happy, I need others to be happy." And "I often worry about others' problems."

When I've used this measure in my studies, I have found that women are significantly more likely than men to say these statements apply to them. I have also found that unmitigated communion is tied to women's tendency to engage in self-focused coping, and to the consequences of self-focused coping.[6] Specifically, women who scored higher on unmitigated communion were more likely to turn inward and ruminate when they were distressed about something. They were also more likely to have symptoms of depression, and to binge eat when upset. In other words, my research suggests that an excessive concern for relationships is a significant contributor to self-focused coping, and in turn to depression and binge eating.

Unmitigated communion, or, more generally, women's concerns about relationships, may contribute to self-focused coping, specifically to symptoms of depression, disordered eating, and heavy drinking in at least three ways.

ALWAYS WATCHING YOURSELF

When you are excessively concerned with how others feel about you and with how your relationships are going, you become extremely self-conscious, always checking yourself and your behaviors to make sure you aren't doing anything that would cause others to disapprove. "Do I look good? Did I say the right thing?" Turning inward, watching and analyzing your every move, you try to ensure that you behave more perfectly in the future. You are hypercritical of yourself for any mistakes you make in your interactions with others. "How could I have said that? What an idiot I am—I should have known not to do that! What must they think of me?"

Unfortunately, mistakes are inevitable and there are always difficult times in relationships. Women beat themselves up for these mistakes and difficulties, losing self-esteem, sometimes becoming sad and depressed. Indeed, when women become so depressed that they need treatment for depression, they most often report that a problematic relationship is at the heart of their suffering. It may be conflict with a spouse. It may be a boss she fears doesn't like her. It may be difficulty in parenting her children. Whatever the relationship problem, women hold themselves responsible for the problem and sink into depression, full of self-criticism and full of terror that the other person may abandon them altogether.

Hannah and Lisa had been best friends since fifth grade. Now, at fifty-two years of age, they were both married with teenage children and had good jobs. They still lived in the same town, so they saw each other at least once a week, for coffee or for a barbecue with both families. It seemed that it was one of those rare friendships that served both women well, and would last their lifetimes.

What most people couldn't see, however, was that Hannah often drove Lisa crazy with her insecurities. If Lisa was having a bad day, and so seemed a bit sour in conversation with Hannah, Hannah would pester her about what was the matter, what had she done to annoy Lisa. Lisa would swear that Hannah had done nothing, that she was just in a bad mood because of something that had happened at work that day, or with the kids. Lisa really just wanted to drop the matter and talk about something else, or attend to cooking dinner. But Hannah kept at her, asking for details about what had happened, trying to "fix" it for her, even if nothing needed fixing. Eventually, Lisa would either just walk away or might blow up at Hannah, telling her just to drop it. If Lisa did blow up, Hannah would seem hurt and confused, saying she had just been trying to be helpful.

Lisa often wondered why she maintained the friendship with Hannah. Sometimes it felt like Hannah was an over-eager puppy, always jumping at her ankles and licking her face. If Lisa got a raise at work, or even just bought a nice new dress, Hannah would praise her until it was embarrassing. Hannah frequently told other people how wonderful it was to have a lifelong relationship with Lisa, how they had been friends since fifth grade, and how close they and their families were to each other. When Lisa thought about pulling away from Hannah and trying to see her less often, she felt extremely guilty, because she knew Hannah would be devastated.

The kind of desperation that Hannah shows in her relationship with Lisa can, as was the case here, drive others away. Even if friends and family members pull away subtly, or try to mask their frustration, women who are excessively concerned about their relationships can sense this, and can become even more desperate in their ploys to maintain the relationship. They exaggerate conflicts that arise, worrying that it means the end. If the end does come, they are devastated, and at risk of falling deep into depression.

EXTREME MAKEOVER

Other women decide that if they could just improve themselves in some way, they could change or hold on to a relationship. This is where excessive dieting sometimes comes in: "I have to lose twenty pounds or my husband will lose interest in me!" Or the woman may try to diet, but lapse into binge eating because her sense of her own body becomes so distorted that she loses control of her eating.

Eating disorders often begin in adolescence. Many theorists argue that they are an attempt by adolescent girls to gain control of their relationships with their families. Theorist Hilde Bruch noted that anorexia nervosa often occurs in girls who have been unusually "good girls," high achievers, dutiful and compliant daughters who are always trying to please their parents and others by being "perfect."[7] These girls tend to have parents who are overinvested in their daughters' compliance and achievements, who are controlling, and who will not allow the expression of feelings, especially negative feelings.

Bruch argued that throughout their daughters' lives these parents were more concerned about their own needs than their daughters' needs for food and comfort. As a result, the daughters do not learn to identify and accept their own feelings and desires but rather to monitor closely the needs and desires of others so as to better comply with others' demands, as we can see in the case of Randi and her family.[8]

> Randi is a sixteen-year-old with anorexia nervosa. Her parents are highly educated and very successful, having spent

most of their careers in the diplomatic corps. Randi, her two brothers, and her parents are "very close, as are many families in the diplomatic corps, because we move so much," although the daily care of the children has always been left to nannies. The children had to follow strict rules for appropriate conduct, both in the home and outside. These rules were partly driven by the requirements of the families of diplomats to "be on their best behavior" in their host country and partly driven by Randi's parents' conservative beliefs. Randi, as the only daughter in the family, always had to behave as "a proper lady" to counteract the stereotype of American girls as brash and sexually promiscuous. All the children were required to act mature beyond their years, controlling any emotional outbursts, taking defeats and disappointments without complaint, and happily picking up and moving every couple of years when their parents were assigned to another country.

Randi's anorexic behaviors began when her parents announced they were leaving the diplomatic corps to return to the United States. Randi had grown very fond of their last post in Europe, because she had finally found a group of friends that she liked and her parents approved of, and she liked her school. She had always done well in school but had often hated the harshly strict schoolteachers. In her present school, she felt accepted by her teachers as well as challenged by the work. When Randi told her parents she would like to finish her last year of high school in this school rather than go to the United States with them, they flatly refused even to consider it. Randi tried to talk with her parents, suggesting she stay with the family of one of her friends, who were willing to have her, but her parents cut her off and told her they would not discuss the idea further. Randi became sullen and withdrawn and stopped eating shortly after the family arrived in the United States.

As a result of family dynamics, Bruch argued, girls who develop anorexia experience themselves as acting in response to others, rather than in response to their own wishes and needs. They don't accurately identify their own feelings and desires, and thus don't cope appropriately with their own distress. They don't even accurately identify their own bodily sensations, such as hunger, contributing to their ability to starve themselves for long periods of time.

Girls in overcontrolling families such as these harbor rage against their families that they can't express. Instead, they discover that controlling their food intake gives them both a sense of control over their lives and elicits concern from their parents. In addition, their rigid control of their bodies provides a sense of power over the whole family, which they never had before.

Research has confirmed that the families of girls with eating disorders tend to experience high levels of conflict, though the expression of negative emotions is discouraged and perfectionism remains a key family theme.[9] These characteristics are also present in the families of girls with depression, and may be one way in which depression and eating disorders are so strongly connected. What may distinguish families in which girls develop eating disorders from those in which girls become depressed is that mothers of girls with eating disorders believe their daughters should lose more weight, are critical of their daughters' weight, or are themselves more likely to have disordered eating patterns.[10]

Drinking Like a Guy

Men tend to drink with their buddies, often as part of "male bonding." Women, however, tend to drink with husbands or boyfriends who hold significant influence over how much they drink. Research shows that married women are prone to matching their husbands' drinking patterns, and when women refuse to drink as much as their husbands, it often creates conflict in the marriage.[11] The problem, of course, is that women can't get away with drinking as much as men.

Diane and Harry had been married twenty-three years. They had grown up together in New Orleans, where their two families had been important in the jazz scene. Diane and Harry had always had an active social life, going to clubs with friends and having dinner parties in their spacious home. Diane loved the vibrant social scene of New Orleans and was known as a generous and creative hostess. She specialized in designing fancy mixed drinks, with exotic juices and lots of alcohol.

Harry was a big man, 6 foot 5, about 250 pounds, and he could drink like a fish. No one ever kept count of how many drinks Harry typically had in a night, least of all Harry, but he always had one in his hand. When they were first married and Diane was in her twenties, she could almost keep up with Harry, though she would invariably have a major hangover the next day after one of their parties or nights at the clubs. Now that she was in her mid-forties, she could only drink about one drink for every two Harry drank. In fact, one reason she began creating new mixed drinks was to keep herself busy at their parties so she wouldn't drink so much. She still drank a lot, however, typically four or five large mixed drinks in an evening, plus maybe some wine or beer.

Every once in a while, Diane would try to cut back and drink much less. But her friends or Harry would tease her about "being on the wagon," or tell her she was making them feel guilty, and push her to drink more. She usually gave in and ordered another drink, vowing that after that night she really was going to cut back on her drinking so she wouldn't feel so lousy after a party.

Trying to drink like a guy starts, unfortunately, early in women's lives. Over 90 percent of girls will have consumed alcohol by the time they graduate high school. Although most adolescent girls drink infrequently and lightly, in the last decade the percentage of high school girls who binge drink has increased so that it is nearly equal to the percentage of high school boys who do so. Teenage binge drinkers consume alcohol with their friends, who also tend to be binge drinkers, and their social life is built around getting drunk together. Schoolwork invariably suffers from their drinking.

College-age women report that they strive to keep up with

male friends' drinking levels at parties, with the expectation that this will impress the guys. Some women drink during the school week in an effort to increase their tolerance levels so they can handle more alcohol on the weekends. My colleague Amy Young, a professor at Eastern Michigan University, has found that "drinking like a guy" is connected in young women's minds to a variant of third-wave feminism, in which college-age women interpret heavy drinking as their right as liberated women.[12] This may be one reason why the rates of health- and life-threatening moderate drinking among young women have spiked significantly in recent decades, and also why there's been a threefold increase in the number of college women who report having been drunk on ten or more occasions in the previous month.

Beauty Queens and Other Dangerous Ideas

Our icons of beauty—the models in glossy magazines, the stars on TV and in the movies, the singing sensations—are getting skinnier and skinnier. Indeed, when researchers tracked the average weight of *Playboy* centerfolds and Miss Americas over the last forty years, they found that the average weight of these women has become much less; by today's standards, these women weigh about 20 percent less than what would be expected for a woman of their height.[13] The average model in a fashion magazine these days is pencil-thin, with a figure that is physically unattainable by the majority of adult women.

Pressure to be thin doesn't come only from the media and

from marketers of Barbie dolls. Women also exert these pressures on one another. We judge women who are thin as more feminine and attractive than those who are heavier, and we judge women who dare to eat as much food as they want in public settings (such as in a dormitory cafeteria) as less attractive than those who eat less.[14] Women pick up on these cues and change their behaviors to conform to social expectations. For example, women eat less in situations where they want to appear desirable and feminine, or in situations in which they want to show superiority over or compete with other women.[15] Just think back for a moment to college or high school, when girls would sit around the cafeteria, watching what each other was eating. Being thin is difficult, however, in our high-fat, fast-food culture. And so girls and women seldom feel they are thin enough, and want to lose more weight.

A PSYCHOLOGICAL CORSET

Can the social pressures toward thinness really lead to symptoms of the toxic triangle in girls and women? Many studies have been done to examine this question, and the answer seems to be yes.[16] Adolescent girls and women who are exposed to persistent messages that they are not thin enough are, not surprisingly, less satisfied with their own appearance. They are also more likely to follow highly restrictive diets, including unhealthy diets. For example, they may restrict themselves to nothing but green salads (no dressing) and herbal tea. It's nearly impossible for people to stay on such restrictive diets, however, and women who feel pressured to be thin are actually more likely to lapse into binge eating. Then they may use purging (vomiting, laxatives, and exercise) to try to lose the weight gained from their binges.

Women who feel pressured to be thin also experience more sadness and symptoms of depression. This sadness and sense of defeat seems to be tied to their dissatisfaction with how their bodies look, as well as to the hopelessness they feel that they will ever be thin enough. Being thin is such a core component of women's and girls' self-esteem these days that failure to achieve this goal can lead to self-loathing and depression.

Even brief exposure to our social icons of beauty is enough to put some women on the road to the toxic triangle. For example, in a study, researchers showed one group of young women images from fashion magazines of ultra-thin models, while another group of young women saw images from nature magazines. Both groups of women saw these images for only three minutes.[17] Those women who saw the ultra-thin models experienced increases in depression, shame, guilt, stress, insecurity, and body dissatisfaction, while those who saw the images from the nature magazines did not. In addition, women who saw the ultra-thin models and who had already subscribed to the thin ideal for women, showed increases in symptoms of bulimia. If just three minutes of exposure to fashion models can have such effects, think what the constant exposure young women experience does to their self-image and well-being!

Another study looked at what chronic exposure to the thin

ideal in fashion magazines does to adolescent girls' mental health.[18] Researchers randomly gave one group of girls, ages thirteen to seventeen, a 15-month subscription to a leading fashion magazine and the other group none. They found that girls who already felt pressured to be thin and who were dissatisfied with their bodies became more depressed over time if they had been given the subscription to the fashion magazine. In addition, girls who had little social support from family members and friends became more dissatisfied with their bodies, dieted more, and showed more bulimic symptoms if they were given the fashion magazine subscription.

Adolescent girls and women can, to some extent, avoid pressures to be thin by avoiding these fashion magazines and other media depictions of the thin ideal. We can't completely avoid our friends, however, and it is sometimes they who are the worst carriers of the thin-ideal message. In another clever study, researchers asked young women students to talk to a young woman whom they thought was just another student but who was actually a confederate or an accomplice in the study. The accomplice was a thin, attractive nineteen-year-old woman, 5 foot 10 inches tall, who weighed 127 pounds.[19] First, both the participant in the study and the accomplice watched a neutral film about a seascape, supposedly so they could rate the film. After the film, the accomplice launched into a pre-scripted conversation with the participant. In the *pressure condition,* the accomplice complained about how dissatisfied she was with her weight and discussed the extreme exercise routine and restrictive diet she was using to reduce. In the *neutral condition,* the accomplice talked about classes she was currently taking and her plans for the weekend. A researcher then entered the room and asked both women to fill out questionnaires about how they felt about their bodies. The participants in the pressure condition became significantly more dissatisfied with their own bodies after talking with the thin accomplice about her own weight concerns. In contrast, the women in the neutral condition did not become more dissatisfied with their bodies after talking with the accomplice about matters unrelated to weight or dieting.

Again, this research shows how much power the messages we get from others about our bodies can hold over us. If just a few minutes of talking with a complete stranger can lead women to become more dissatisfied with their bodies, think what hearing these messages from an admired peer can do a young woman's self-perception!

EATING AND DRINKING GO TOGETHER

You'd think that women who are highly concerned about their weight would avoid alcohol because it is highly caloric. Research shows, however, that women who are dissatisfied with their bodies and subscribe to the thin ideal use alcohol more frequently than women who are more satisfied with their bodies or who reject the thin ideal.[20] Though not much is known about why this is, it may be that women who want to be thin but can't attain this goal become depressed, and so use alcohol to relieve the symptoms of depression.[21] It may also be that women use alcohol to escape the chronic self-consciousness created by pressure to be thin. Finally, constantly restraining yourself from eating in an effort to be thin can make you vulnerable to all sorts of impulsive behavior, including binge eating and binge drinking.

> *The woman we met at the beginning of this book, Jill, began her yo-yo eating patterns as an adolescent in response to an accumulation of pressures from her family. Her heavy drinking emerged in college. Jill's parents were both overweight, due in part to their family meals of heavy, fattening foods in large portions. Jill was never terribly heavy herself, although she inherited the pear shape of her father's side of the family, carrying much of her weight in her rear end and hips. Her father, who was not the most sensitive guy in the world, would tease her about having a "tub butt." Jill would try to diet and lose weight, but her mother pushed her to eat at meals. It was during this time that Jill developed the habit of avoiding eating for long periods, then eating heavily when pressured by her mother.*
>
> *When Jill went to college, she discovered how much she liked alcohol. Being intoxicated was a welcome relief from the pressure to do well in school. Her accomplishments, however, were never really enough for her parents, who were quick to criticize but slow to praise. Losing herself in alcohol gave her a short respite from her own self-criticism and worries about failing. Of course, being hungover two or three times a week made it that much harder to keep up with her schoolwork.*

The social pressures on women to be thin, to be concerned with relationships above all else, and to suppress anger and frustration in favor of sadness and fear are clearly not the only contributors to the toxic triangle. Although most, if not all, women are exposed to these pressures, most women, fortunately, do not develop significant psychological symptoms. Nonetheless, the toxic atmosphere that these pressures create keeps women's focus on their bodies—on how they look to others as well as how able they are to control their appearance—which contributes to self-focused coping and nudges them down the path into the toxic triangle.[22]

FOUR

=▼=

Our Bodies Conspire against Us

WE'VE SEEN THAT the social conditions and expectations that women face can lead them to cope with their problems in ways that make them vulnerable to depressive symptoms, yo-yo eating, and heavy drinking. These same social conditions may also have a part in shaping women's biological responses to stress in ways that compound these maladies, drawing women further into the toxic triangle. The conditions in which women live can have a large hand in their biological reactions to stress, speeding them into the toxic triangle.

The Permanent Scars of Early Trauma

A fascinating and critically important new line of research suggests that traumatic experiences early in life can cause permanent changes in the response of the brain and body to stress, which in turn can heighten sensitivity to each of the components of the toxic triangle. The brain and body have a natural response to stress that was put in place over the course of evolution. Our heart rate, blood pressure, and breathing rate increase, our muscles tense, saliva and mucus dry up, increasing the size of air passages to our lungs, while at the same time certain unessential activities, such as digestion, slow down. The body's natural painkillers, endorphins, are secreted and our surface blood vessels constrict to reduce bleeding in case of injury. This automatic physiological response to stress is known as the *fight-or-flight response*.

These physiological changes begin when the brain recognizes a threat and activates the biological circuitry of fear. An area of the brain called the hypothalamus initiates the release of a number of hormones, including adrenocorticotropic hormone (ACTH), the body's major stress hormone. ACTH stimulates the release of another group of hormones, the major one being cortisol. The amount of cortisol in blood or urine samples is often used as a measure of stress. Eventually, this group of hormones signals the hippocampus, a part of the brain that helps regulate emotions, to turn off this physiological cascade of hormones when the threat has passed.

Problems in the functioning of the fight-or-flight response have been linked to a number of mental health problems, most frequently depression and anxiety. People with serious depression or anxiety disorders tend to have either exaggerated or blunted fight-or-flight responses to new stressors—it's as if their bodies overreact to the stressors and can't shut off the physiological fight-or-flight response when a stressor has passed, or their fight-or-flight response never gets activated adequately when they are faced by stress. Poor functioning of the fight-or-flight response can also lead to changes in appetite and cravings for alcohol and other drugs.[1]

Psychologist Dante Cicchetti of the University of Rochester, New York, has shown that children who are chronically abused or neglected show significant changes in the functioning of this fight-or-flight response.[2] Depending on the kind of stress they have been exposed to and its duration, this fight-or-flight response is either overreactive or underreactive. The result is that their bodies and minds don't adapt well to new stress. They have trouble turning off their fears, which keeps them going in difficult times, or controlling impulsive behaviors.

Similarly, researcher Christine Heim and her colleagues at Emory University in Atlanta have found that women who were sexually abused as children show abnormal fight-or-flight responses to new stressors as adults, even when they are not currently suffering from symptoms of depression, anxiety, or other mental health problems.[3] For example, in one study, Heim and colleagues recruited 49 women, some who had a history of childhood sexual abuse, and some who did not.[4] The women came to

Heim's laboratory, were asked to sit in front of a panel of three judges and a video camera, and then give a five-minute speech on their qualifications for an open job position. The women were then asked to subtract the number 13 from 2,083, and then subtract 13 from the resulting number, and so on, as quickly and accurately as possible; if they made a mistake they were told to start again from the beginning. This mental arithmetic task went on for five minutes. After these laboratory stressors, the researchers drew blood from each of the women to determine their levels of the stress hormones ACTH and cortisol.

The women who had been abused as children had significantly higher levels of ACTH and cortisol in their blood after the stressful experience in the lab compared to the women who had not been abused, whether or not either group was depressed or anxious at the time of the study. Essentially, this suggests that women who have been abused have a sensitized fight-or-flight response, which may overreact to new stressors.

Chronic overreaction of the fight-or-flight response can lead not only to symptoms of depression, unhealthy eating, and alcohol craving—it can also damage the brain.[5] Animals exposed to significant stress (such as being separated from their mothers as infants) have chronically activated stress responses and, in turn, show a number of changes in the structure and functioning of their brains. The hippocampus, involved in the stress response, shrinks. The functioning of the prefrontal cortex, which is critically important in our ability to choose and control our behaviors in response to stress, is also compromised. Many different circuits in the brain appear to be permanently affected by a chronically activated stress response, including the circuits that regulate brain chemicals such as serotonin and adrenaline. The animals in these studies show signs of being in a toxic triangle of their own—they become unmotivated, seem mopey and sad, lose their appetite, and, if allowed to, drink more alcohol.

Though it remains difficult to look inside the brains of living humans to see if similar changes take place in response to chronic or severe stress, modern neuroimaging techniques, such as MRI and PET scans, are affording a better view of the human brain than we've ever had before. Studies using these technologies are finding that adults who have had traumatic childhood experiences such as physical or sexual abuse also show reductions in the volume of their hippocampus and changes in the functioning of their prefrontal cortex, just as in animals exposed to severe stress.[6] This suggests that early experiences of abuse can create changes in humans' brains that make them more vulnerable to stress, just as early traumas can change animals' brains for the worse. Some studies of abused children suggest that brain changes may remain incipient until chronic stress over the course of childhood and adolescence triggers the activation of the fight-or-flight response caused by that stress, causing permanent changes in the brain.

Does this mean that women who have been abused or neglected as children have no hope of escaping these changes in their brains and avoiding depression, eating disorders, and heavy drinking? No! Because the human brain is flexible, even devastating histories of trauma can be overcome. Charles Nemeroff, Christine Heim, and their colleagues have shown that depressed women with a history of serious abuse as children responded well to a form of psychotherapy that helped them learn to cope better with stress, called Cognitive Behavioral Analysis System of Psychotherapy (CBASP).[7] Indeed, this psychotherapy was more effective in lifting women's depressions than was medication (a common antidepressant called Serzone). Other studies have shown that depressed people who respond well to cognitive therapies such as CBASP show changes for the better in the functioning of their brain.[8] These same therapies are also highly effective in treating eating and alcohol problems.

We can go back to animal studies again to see that early traumatic experiences do not necessarily doom the brain to permanent damage. It turns out that little rat pups who have been traumatized by being separated from their mothers can escape long-term effects of this trauma on their brains and bodies if they are given a great deal of love and care by an adoptive mother rat.[9] Similarly, monkeys who are exposed to severe stress as infants can avoid permanent biological changes and lifelong mental health problems if they are placed in nurturing adoptive homes.

So the brain can change in ways that overcome the effects of early stress. In the last chapters of this book, I will discuss how to use modern psychotherapy and self-help techniques to overcome the effects of early traumas and protect against further susceptibility to the toxic triangle.

It's in Your Genes

It's clear that genetics plays an important role in the likelihood that you will suffer severe versions of each of the three components of the toxic triangle: depression, disordered eating, and excessive drinking. How do we know this? First, all three disorders run in families, so if a parent has had one, you are at greater risk to develop not just that disorder but any one of the three components of the toxic triangle. For example, one study of 5,877 adults from all over the United States found that if a parent had major depression, his or her adult children were 2.73 times more likely to have major depression and 1.68 times more likely to have an alcohol disorder than if the parent did not have depression.[10] In a study I've been working on with psychologists Robert Zucker of the University of Michigan and Hiram Fitzgerald of Michigan State University, the children of parents who were alcoholics had a much greater rate of alcohol-related problems and depressive symptoms than the children of parents who were not alcoholics. Marcy's story illustrates how the toxic triangle can come together in families.

Marcy's dad, Jim, was one of those skinny alcoholics. He drank most of his meals, and was chronically pale and undernourished, so that his 6-foot-2-inch frame was mostly skin and bones. Jim was also a quiet, probably depressed, alcoholic. He never got loud or mean when he drank. In fact, he rarely talked much to anyone, including his family members.

He just sat in the family room watching TV in the dark, drinking beer, from the time he got home from work in the midafternoon to after midnight. You could hardly see him except for the glow of his cigarette and the reflection of the TV light off his dirty white T-shirt.

Marcy's mom, on the other hand, wasn't so skinny. She coped with Jim's alcoholism and her own feelings of isolation and depression by eating. She was endlessly on a diet, but it never did much good; she usually rebounded to weigh even more than she had before she began the diet. She cooked meals for Marcy and the other children in the family, and kept the house, but rarely went anywhere, including to Marcy's school functions, because she was ashamed of herself.

For many of her growing-up years, Marcy tried to believe that it didn't matter to her that her mother and father were largely self-absorbed and absent from her life. But she seldom brought friends home because she was embarrassed by her dad. She tried to ignore her parents and get involved in her schoolwork and friends. This became much harder, however, when she entered high school. The pressures of school and the prospect of dating became more than she could bear. She found her moods becoming morbid; her energy dwindled, as did her self-esteem. She felt ugly and thought she should lose weight. She tried alcohol and marijuana at a party, and found she liked them—even craved them—to a frightening degree.

Maybe it is the environment that parents create in their homes and not their genes that cause their children to be at increased risk for the toxic triangle. Certainly, Marcy wasn't getting a lot of support from her parents, nor were they acting as great role models for how to cope with stress.

Researchers often use twins in studies to try to tease apart the effects of environment from genetics. Twin studies also help to control for the effects of environment because both twins are raised by the same parents, whether identical or fraternal. In a twin study, we first identify all the individuals who have a particular disorder. Then we determine whether his or her twin also has the disorder. Identical twins have exactly the same genetic makeup, so if a disorder is caused entirely by genetics, both twins should have the disorder 100 percent of the time. Fraternal twins have only about 50 percent of their genes in common, just as any two siblings with the same biological parents do, so even in the case of a purely genetic disorder, when one twin is affected, the other twin should have the disorder much less than 100 percent of the time.

Twin studies provide evidence that genes play a role in all three components of the toxic triangle. For example, one study of 2,163 pairs of female twins found that among identical twins, when one twin had bulimia, the other twin had bulimia 26 percent of the time. But among fraternal twins, when one twin had bulimia, the other twin had bulimia only 16 percent of the time.[11] When one identical twin had alcohol problems, the other twin also had alcohol problems 47 percent of the time, but when one fraternal twin had alcohol problems, the other twin had such problems only 32 percent of the time.[12] The differences in incidence of major depression in female identical and fraternal twins is not as large: when an identical twin had major depression, her co-twin also had depression 48 percent of the time; when a fraternal twin had depression, her co-twin had depression 43 percent of the time.[13]

This dizzying array of probabilities shows two things. First, genes play a role in vulnerability to these disorders. We know this because identical twins are always more likely than fraternal twins to have the disorder if one twin has it. Second, genes don't explain everything about vulnerability to these disorders. If they did, then when one twin has the disorder, her identical twin should have it 100 percent of the time, but this isn't the case.

Even more relevant to understanding why some women are prone to fall into the toxic triangle is the evidence that the *same* genes are involved in vulnerability to the three members of the triangle. Here the statistics get more complicated, but in essence, researchers use the same kinds of twin studies to determine to what extent the co-occurrence of all three members of the toxic triangle is due to genetics. The bottom line in these studies is that depression and eating disorders share some of the same genes.[14] Similarly, depression and heavy drinking share some of the same genes.[15] In other words, the same genes appear to increase your risk for both depression and eating disorders. And another set of genes appears to increase your risk for both depression and heavy drinking. The evidence for a genetic component in the co-occurrence of alcohol disorders and eating disorders is less clear.[16]

Although a few early studies have suggested that both disorders had some of the same genes in common, more recent studies, which were larger and more methodologically sound, did not.[17]

As we've seen, genes alone don't lead women into the toxic triangle; instead, it is the conspiracy of disordered genes and severe stress that sends some women down this path. This was shown in an ambitious study conducted by researchers Avshalom Caspi, Terri Moffitt, and colleagues at the University of Wisconsin and the Institute of Medicine in London. They followed a group of 1,037 people from age three to twenty-six, interviewing them every few years to determine the state of their mental health.[18] They found that a particular abnormal gene put people at risk for depression, but only if they also experienced significant life stress, such as maltreatment as a child, unemployment, or the breakup of a close relationship.

The same kinds of studies have not been done with eating and alcohol problems, but many researchers believe that similar models hold true. It takes the combination of vulnerable genes and certain life experiences to push a woman over the edge into the toxic triangle.

It's in Your Head:
The Role of Brain Chemistry

How would genes predispose some women to the toxic triangle? Genes guide the development of the brain, and thus can lead to malfunctions in the brain, contributing to the development of the toxic triangle. In particular, genes play a critical role in the func-tioning of chemicals in our brains that help to regulate our moods and behaviors.

SEROTONIN

You are probably familiar with the theory that depression is caused by too little serotonin in the brain. Serotonin is a neurotransmitter—a chemical that helps the brain transmit mes-sages from one area to another. Serotonin is important to the smooth functioning of many areas of the brain, including those involved with moods, appetite and eating patterns, and the ability to control our impulses.

The idea that depression is caused by too little serotonin is probably simplistic, but it does appear that depressed people have problems in the functioning of the serotonin systems in their brains.[19] The most popular depression medications, sero-tonin reuptake inhibitors like Prozac, Zoloft, and Paxil, regulate levels of serotonin in the brain.

Serotonin is also important in pathological eating behavior. Women with bulimia or anorexia tend to show deficiencies in their levels of serotonin.[20] These deficiencies may cause the body to crave carbohydrates, which women with bulimia often binge on. Women with bulimia take up vomiting or other purging be-haviors in an attempt to control their weight. In women with anorexia, deficiencies in serotonin may interfere with the mes-sages they get from different parts of the brain, particularly the hypothalamus, which tell them whether they are hungry or not.[21] Because they are not able to get these messages clearly, they are capable of starving themselves for the sake of pursuing their ideal of thinness.

Serotonin is also important in drinking behavior because it influences our ability to control impulsive behavior.[22] Binge drinking is the result of breakdowns in the ability to inhibit or control your impulses. Imbalances in serotonin may lead us to a variety of impulsive behaviors, including binge drinking, binge eating, and suicidal behavior.

These different lines of evidence suggest that improper functioning of serotonin systems in the brain may be crucial in the development of depression, pathological eating, and heavy drinking, and also in more moderate symptoms of each of these.

Dopamine

Another important brain chemical is dopamine. The brain appears to have its own "pleasure pathway" that affects our experience of reward.[23] Rich in neurons sensitive to the neurotransmitter dopamine, this pathway is activated by natural rewards, such as the taste of good food and the physical pleasure that goes along with sexual stimulation. The same pathway is activated much more intensely by substances such as alcohol, that can be abused or on which a dependency can be developed. The activation of the pleasure pathway in the brain actually leads people to want to repeat the events that caused its activation—for instance, when a small bite of tasty food whets your appetite, or when a sip of alcohol causes the desire for another sip.

When the pleasure pathway is activated by a substance like alcohol, the brain may try to balance this state of activation with processes that have opposite effects. These opposing processes may remain active even after a woman stops drinking the alcohol, and may cause many of the symptoms of withdrawal.

The chronic use of substances such as alcohol may produce permanent changes in the pleasure pathway, causing a craving even after withdrawal symptoms pass. The more a woman uses alcohol, the more the dopamine neurons in her pleasure pathway become hyperactive, or sensitized. This sensitization can be permanent, so that the neurons will be activated even more greatly the next time she drinks. This creates a chronic and strong craving for alcohol, which makes it very difficult to resist drinking. Similarly, hypersensitivity of the dopamine neurons may place women at risk for any behavior that activates this pleasure pathway, including binge eating.[24]

Depression involves a loss of the ability to enjoy pleasure, to enjoy much about life. Deficiencies in dopamine in the pleasure pathway may lead to the cardinal symptoms of depression. One of the newest and most promising methods of treating depression, repetitive transcranial magnetic stimulation (rTMS) may work by enhancing levels of dopamine.[25] In rTMS, patients are exposed to powerful magnets such as those in magnetic resonance imagery (MRI) machines. Repeated high-intensity magnetic pulses are focused on particular brain structures. Several studies have suggested that depressed patients given rTMS daily for at least a week experience relief from their symptoms.[26]

Your Hormones and You

We can't have a discussion of women's biology and how it affects their mental health without talking about hormones. Actually, we've talked about hormones already in this chapter—fight-or-flight response involves the release of a number of critical hormones, including cortisol. But the specific hormones that everyone thinks of when it comes to women's mental health are the so-called female hormones.

One clue that hormones play a role in the toxic triangle is that the triangle doesn't exist before puberty. The rates of depression, eating disorders, or alcohol problems among girls (or boys, for that matter) are very low before about age thirteen. Then, somewhere in the early adolescent years, rates of depression and eating problems skyrocket in girls, and drinking begins.[27] Certainly not all adolescent girls become depressed or develop eating or drinking problems. Indeed, only the minority do. But early adolescence is a critical time when girls who are going to develop these problems usually begin to do so.

Is the onset of the toxic triangle in some early-adolescent girls due to the hormonal changes of puberty? That question is hard to answer. One study of over a thousand nine- to thirteen-year-olds found a correlation between levels of estradiol and depressed mood in girls.[28] But most studies have not found any

direct relationship between specific hormones and mood or behavior problems in girls.[29]

The normal hormonal changes of puberty may only trigger
depression, eating disorders, and alcohol problems in girls with
genetic or other biological vulnerabilities. Hormones can affect
the functioning of neurotransmitters that regulate mood and behavior, including serotonin. Estrogen can also affect the biological stress response discussed earlier in this chapter.[30] In girls who
have a genetic vulnerability to depression, eating disorders, or alcohol problems, the normal hormonal changes of puberty may
cause problems in the functioning of their neurotransmitters,
triggering symptoms of these disorders. If this is correct, it would
mean that only biologically vulnerable girls would show a relationship between hormones and their moods and drinking and
eating behaviors. One study of adolescent twins supported this
idea, showing that a genetic vulnerability to depression was triggered by puberty for girls.[31]

Some studies have found that the *timing* of puberty, rather
than a specific stage of puberty, affects girls' vulnerability to the
toxic triangle. Girls who go through the major changes of puberty, such as getting their periods, developing breasts, or gaining
weight, several months before their girlfriends, are more likely
than girls who mature around the same time as their girlfriends
to show depression, eating disorders, and alcohol abuse.[32] For
boys, maturing earlier than your peer group doesn't afford the
same risk for mental health problems as it does for girls.

The reasons for differences between girls and boys in the impact of pubertal timing are not entirely clear, but they may have

to do with the social meanings associated with those changes. Girls are much more likely than boys to dislike the physical changes that accompany puberty, particularly because they gain weight and lose the lithe, prepubescent look idealized in modern fashions. Girls who get their periods considerably earlier than their peers (say in fifth grade) are particularly dissatisfied and unhappy with their bodies.[33] In turn, several studies have shown that a higher incidence of negative body image in girls contributes to increased levels of depressive symptoms and eating disorders in girls compared to boys.[34]

Jill, whose story we have been following in previous chapters, hit puberty in the sixth grade. Or maybe we should say that puberty hit Jill. It seemed as if overnight her body plumped up and her breasts began to bulge out of her clothes.

Jill had never cared much about her weight in elementary school. She was small and athletic, a forward on her school's soccer team. She wasn't as fast as some of the taller girls, but her ball-handling skills were fantastic, and her little brown body could dart around almost any player she opposed.

But with her new body, Jill didn't know what to do on the soccer field. She felt heavy and slow, as though she couldn't control the ball as she used to. Jill also felt fat compared to the other girls in her class, most of whom were still skinny as rails and flat-chested. She began to wear loose, bulky clothes to try to hide her size, but these made her look even more dumpy. Unfortunately, this was about the time that her father began to call her "tub butt."

This was also when Jill started to skip meals in an effort to lose weight. She made excuses to her mother about needing to go to school early to study, or to soccer practice in the evenings, so that she could avoid both breakfast and dinner. If her mother packed her a lunch, she would throw most of it away. She found she could ignore her hunger pretty well, although she was often dizzy and tired. She lost some weight, but not nearly enough to suit her, so she became more and more embarrassed by her appearance. She quit the soccer team, because much of the time she was too drained and light-headed to run and play, and because she didn't want to be seen in shorts.

Girls are also likely to experience depression and eating problems during puberty if they face stressful events such as having to switch schools at the same time their bodies are undergoing major changes. Anne Petersen and colleagues from Pennsylvania State University found that girls who moved from elementary to junior high school within six months of the onset of menstruation and other major pubertal changes had significantly more depressive symptoms in junior high and remained at higher levels of depressive symptoms in twelfth grade.[35] Boys didn't show the same effects—the co-occurrence of pubertal change and school change wasn't associated with depressive symptoms in them. This may be because boys embrace their pubertal changes and are consequently less reactive than girls to stressful events that occur during puberty.

Girls who mature early can also have very different social lives than girls who mature later.[36] Early-maturing girls tend to start dating at a younger age and are more likely to become sexually active at a young age. Unfortunately, this puts them at increased risk for date rape and other forms of sexual abuse and coercion, which in turn increases their risk for depression, eating disorders, and alcohol problems. In addition, early-maturing girls tend to date older boys, who are more likely to introduce them to alcohol and drug use.

Oxytocin: The Other Hormone

Another hormone that plays an important role in women's lives, though not as well understood as estrogen or progesterone, is oxytocin. This hormone stimulates milk ejection when breast-feeding and uterine contractions during childbirth and has been shown in studies with animals to play a role in *affiliative behaviors*—patterns of building close relationships with others. In animals, oxytocin is important in triggering caregiving behaviors by mothers toward infants and in females' bonding with their sexual partners. A number of researchers have argued that oxytocin also plays a role in affiliative behaviors in humans.

Psychologist Jill Cyranowski of the University of Pittsburgh and her colleagues suggest that increases in oxytocin activity in girls during puberty lead them to become more affiliative—to care more about relationships with others, to become more caring toward others, and to desire to be with and be liked by others, especially their peers.[37] This in itself is not toxic; indeed, it's probably programmed into females by evolution. It is adaptive for females to become more affiliative when they become able to bear children. It makes them want to mate with males, and it makes them want to give nurturance and care to their offspring.

But an increase in affiliative desire and behavior can be toxic when it interacts with three other risk factors that can also occur during girls' transition to adolescence. The first of these is an insecure relationship with parents. Girls who are securely attached to their parents can weather the transition to adolescence well. They have support when negative events, such as the breakup of a relationship, happens. They can use their parents as a safe base and source of advice as they make decisions about relationships and activities.

But girls with poor relationships with their parents don't have this resource. They may prematurely turn to romantic and sexual relationships to get the love and support they are not getting from their parents. Early romantic relationships tend to be unstable, even potentially dangerous, which can increase a girl's risk for sexual exploitation. Some girls become depressed over these relationships and may engage in unhealthy eating behaviors in an attempt to control their bodies and their relationships. Some may get involved in alcohol if their boyfriends lead them in that direction, as did Sheri.

Sheri was a pretty girl, 5 foot 6 and about 130 pounds, with long blond hair and her mother's Nordic looks. She never felt very pretty, though, like the popular girls who were really skinny and had great clothes. So when, during the eighth grade, a boy named Ryan began showing some interest in her, Sheri was both surprised and thrilled. Sheri knew her parents wouldn't approve of Ryan, because his parents didn't have as much money or social status as Sheri's parents did. But Sheri couldn't care less. The fact that her father was president of the city council and her mother was one of the most successful real estate agents in town only meant that she rarely saw them, and Sheri felt they didn't care about her or her activities. She knew if her mother found out about Ryan, she would just scream at Sheri and forbid her to see him, without letting Sheri say a word in her own defense. So Sheri kept Ryan a secret from her parents.

Ryan always seemed to know where the parties were— the ones hosted by older kids who had easy access to alcohol and sometimes drugs. On nights when her parents were at city council meetings and real estate showings, Sheri would sneak out with Ryan and go to these parties. At first, she didn't drink much. She felt dizzy after she had some alcohol and nearly threw up in front of Ryan. She couldn't bear the thought of embarrassing herself in front of him, or doing anything that might drive him away. But gradually she got accustomed to the alcohol and could drink more and more of it without getting too dizzy. She was usually more drunk than she would admit, however, slurring her words and stumbling around. When Ryan groped her, she would try to make jokes and gently push him off, but occasionally she just passed out, and didn't know exactly what had happened while she was unconscious.

Her hangovers the next day were interfering with her schoolwork and her grades were dropping. This prompted a screaming session with her mother. When she was younger, Sheri would just sit and take this abuse. Now, however, she started screaming back at her mother, using swear words, and stormed out of the room. Her mother declared that Sheri was grounded, but Sheri just told her mother to "F——off" as she stomped up to her bedroom.

Sheri fully expected to sneak out that night to be with Ryan, but he called early in the evening to say he had something else he had to do and wouldn't be seeing her. Sheri panicked—what did this mean, was he seeing someone else, did she do something to drive him away?! It turned out that her fears were justified—Ryan had met another girl at one of the parties where Sheri had passed out, and had become more interested in her than in Sheri.

Over the next month, it became clear to Sheri that the relationship with Ryan was finished. She was devastated. She locked herself in her room and refused to go to school. No amount of yelling by her mother could get Sheri to talk about what had happened.

Increase in the desire to be with peers can become toxic when it interacts with a particular type of personality or temperament known as an *anxious temperament*. Some girls, and boys, are born highly reactive, anxious, and socially inhibited. This temperament seems to be due, in part, to genes. It can lead to insecure relationships with parents and to difficulties in peer relationships. Girls with anxious temperaments may be inhibited about forming relationships with others, although they want them at least as much as other girls, and may suffer emotionally as a consequence of not having them. Or girls may get involved in unhealthy behaviors, like excessive dieting or binge drinking, in an effort to overcome their inhibitions and "fit in."

Affiliation can also become toxic when combined with selffocused coping, discussed earlier in this book. Girls who enter the stormy years of early adolescence with changes in their attitudes toward others and a tendency toward self-focused coping can have difficulty making safe and healthy choices for themselves. It is that much harder to bounce back from the inevitable bumps in the road that come with this period of life.

Each of these three risk factors—insecure relationships with parents, an anxious or inhibited temperament, and self-focused coping—puts girls at risk for mood and behavioral problems during the transition into adolescence. But in combination with the natural increase in the desire to form close interpersonal ties spawned by increases in oxytocin, there is a significant increase in risk for mood and behavioral problems in girls. As we know, a young adolescent girl desperately wants to be loved and accepted by others, especially by her peers. If she doesn't have a secure parental relationship or effective coping skills and is temperamentally anxious, this increase in desire for relationships can cause her to turn to the wrong people or activities. In turn, when problems in relationships come, as they inevitably do, she may be more likely to become depressed and may turn to disordered eating or alcohol abuse in an attempt to self-medicate or gain the favor of others.

It's probably not the case that biology leads directly to the toxic triangle. Instead, biology can set up vulnerabilities in girls and women so that, when confronted by certain social conditions, these vulnerabilities are triggered, adding to a girl's stress to the point that she begins to travel the path to the toxic triangle.

FIVE

Thinking Our Way into the Toxic Triangle

Pʀᴇssuʀᴇs ᴛᴏ ʙᴇ thin, caring, and empathic toward others, and to cope quietly and internally with stress, lead some women to develop ways of thinking about themselves and the world that can further set them on the path to the toxic triangle. These thinking styles, or ways of processing information, keep women focused on controlling their bodies and minds as a way of coping, instead of acting to change societal norms and the pressures they face as a result of them.

Overthinking

When something distressing happens, like getting a pay cut on the job, it's natural to think about it. We turn it over in our minds, analyzing the situation. Should we file a grievance? Change jobs? Many of us decide there isn't anything we can do, and move on; some decide to take some action to make the situation better. For example, we might come to the conclusion that since everyone else has gotten a pay cut, there is little we can do about it, and since we don't want to change jobs right now, we'll just have to live with less money. Or we might decide to immediately apply to a new job because in fact the pay cut is outrageously unjustified.

But some of us have a hard time doing either. We roll potential decisions over in our minds, again, and again, and again. We question the motives of the people involved—how could our boss be so mean? We look for a deeper meaning in the situation—is there something about me that means I can't find a stable job? We worry about the future—what if I can't live within this lower salary, or can't find a better-paying job? We connect this situation to ones that have happened in the past—my last two jobs were with companies that had to downsize, it's just not fair!

I have labeled this process of going over and over a situation and the feelings it provokes, rehashing things that have happened before, worrying about the future, being unable to make decisions in the present, as *overthinking*. In my book *Women Who Think Too Much,* I described dozens of women who get stuck overthinking. They can't let go of past events, constantly rework or "relive" them, trying to understand their meaning and implication for their lives. Fretting about things that haven't happened yet, they anticipate the worst and consequently become immobilized when they try to make decisions.

Jenna, a twenty-six-year-old junior marketing executive for a major firm on the East Coast, is a rabid overthinker whose bouts can cover vast territory—her work, her family, her love life—but the most common focus is her body, and how much she eats and drinks. Let's listen to some of the thoughts that go through her head.

I can't believe I lost control so completely last night at that reception for our office! I'd been doing so well on the promises I made to myself to eat healthily and not drink. I should have been able to keep control, even though the food was spectacular and the wine was free. Instead, I ate like a pig— I must have consumed a thousand calories! And I'm not even sure how many glasses of wine I had! I know it was enough to make me feel lousy today!

I'm just a weakling. I always seem to lose control no matter how hard I try. I can't keep my promises to myself in other areas of my life, either. I'm not exercising like I should. I'm not keeping in touch with old friends like I said I would. What's wrong with me? Why can't I do even these simple things?

I'm never going to find a guy if I can't get a grip on myself. No wonder I can't keep a relationship going for very long. What guy would want a woman who can't control herself around food and wine? I saw that guy, Sam, from the accounting department sneering at me last night. He probably thought I was disgusting standing by the table just shoveling the food in and guzzling the wine down.

Oh, I hope my boss, Karen, didn't notice me last night.

I'm having a hard enough time impressing her on the job—I don't need her to think I'm a drunk. What if she saw me? Should I say something to her, apologize or something? But then she might take my defensiveness as a sign that I really do have a drinking problem. And what if she didn't see me? I don't want to say anything if she didn't see me! Okay, who was there standing near the table last night that I can trust? Is there someone I can ask if Karen was anywhere near while I was chowing down at the food table?

Jenna might have had reason for concern if she actually had been standing by the table gorging herself on food and gulping down alcohol—but that's not what she did. She took a reasonable plate of food and a glass of wine and stood there talking with coworkers as she ate and drank. Thanks to overthinking, this plate of food and glass of wine turned into an orgy of eating and drinking. Now Jenna—again thanks to overthinking—is making matters worse by anxiously talking with coworkers about her exaggerated memory of her own behavior.

Overthinking doesn't just make us have unwise conversations with our coworkers. In twenty years of research, I have found that overthinking can also lead to significant mental health problems.[1] The first is depression. My students and I have conducted several studies in which we have tracked overthinkers and non-overthinkers for a period of a year or two. We have found that overthinkers are significantly more likely to develop moderate symptoms of depression, and even to be diagnosed with a depressive disorder, than are non-overthinkers.

Overthinking leads to depression in several ways. First, when you overthink, you are looking for trouble—you dredge up problems and bad memories from the past, you focus on obstacles in your current situation, you worry about the future. These negative thoughts tear you down, make you feel hopeless, helpless, and depressed.

Second, overthinking gets in the way of doing what you can to take control of your problems and feel better. Although women often enter into bouts of overthinking because they are trying to understand problems they'd like to solve, overthinking actually interferes with good problem solving. It's harder to generate good solutions to problems when you are overthinking. I showed this in an experiment I conducted with Sonja Lyubomirsky, now a professor of psychology at University of California, Riverside.[2]

Sonja and I invited two groups of moderately depressed people to participate. In one group, we encouraged them to begin overthinking (by directing their attention to the kinds of thoughts that overthinkers get stuck on). In the other group, we encouraged them not to overthink, by giving them pleasantly distracting scenes on which to focus (such as a fan slowly turning on a warm day, or a bird gliding overhead). We then gave everyone in the study a difficult interpersonal problem, such as a friend who is avoiding you, and asked them how they would solve it. The participants in the overthinking group generated solutions that were significantly less effective than those in the pleasant distractions group. For example, the overthinkers' "solutions" included "I guess I'd just avoid my friend too." In contrast, the people in the distraction group came up with solutions such as "I'd gently ask my friend if I'd done anything to offend her." When you are over-thinking, you may feel you're gaining great insights into your problems, but you're actually working at a disadvantage in terms of problem solving. As a result, problems don't go away, they just get worse, which can make you depressed. ·

Third, overthinking annoys other people. With psychologist Christopher Davis, who is now at Carleton College in Ottawa, Ontario, I did a study in which we tracked, for two years, over-thinkers and non-overthinkers after they had endured the death of a close family member (usually an elderly parent or spouse).[3] The overthinkers reached out to others for social support more than the non-overthinkers, which makes sense. Because over-thinkers had so much on their minds, they wanted to share their thoughts and concerns with trusted friends and family members. But over time, the overthinkers reported that people pulled away from them, and even became hostile. In essence, the overthinkers were violating social rules about how long one should actively grieve a loss—they were thinking and talking about their loss and their feelings way beyond the time when their family mem-bers and friends felt they should have moved on. As a conse-quence, friends and family members became increasingly frustrated with the overthinkers, telling them to "get over it" or "get a grip." Now, this response may not be fair. Nevertheless, the end result was that the overthinkers lost social support at a time when they still needed it badly, and were much more likely than non-overthinkers to have serious symptoms of depression over the two years we followed them.

Some overthinkers try to escape the roar of their thoughts by binge eating or binge drinking. In a questionnaire study I did with 735 adults randomly chosen from the San Francisco Bay community, I found that overthinkers were significantly more likely than non-overthinkers to binge eat and drink when they were upset. A good example is Marina, a thirty-four-year-old freelance computer consultant, with deep brown eyes and long blond hair.

> *Marina's overthinking bouts usually began with a disagreement with her husband, Perry. Their marriage was actually fairly solid and happy, but he could become quite unreasonable when he was in a bad mood and would say things that just sent Marina's thoughts flying. She could go from disagreement to wanting to file for divorce in just an hour of overthinking!*
>
> *One night Perry came home from a business trip, and after a brief hello to Marina and their son, Jason, said, "You two need to stop burning so many lights at night—our electric bill is through the roof!"*
>
> *Marina fumed about this remark for hours, particularly as she lay in bed that night. "How could he be so hostile and focus on such a trivial thing when we hadn't seen him for days? What kind of jerk is he?! Why do I put up with this?"*
>
> *But her thoughts were not only (justifiably) angry thoughts at her husband. They also spread and grew as her overthinking fueled them: "Sometimes I think I should just leave him. At least then I wouldn't have to put up with his rudeness. And Jason wouldn't have to be the target of his*

hostility either. But I can't leave him, I wouldn't have enough money for Jason and me to live comfortably. And I'm not sure I could live without him, or at least without some husband. I don't want to be a single parent. Why does he think he can get away with treating me like this? I don't think he cares what I think anymore. He doesn't seem to be attracted to me much—he hardly ever initiates sex. What should I do? What can I do?"

At about 1 A.M., Marina got out of bed and wandered down to the kitchen, overwhelmed by her thoughts and wanting some relief from her anxiety and sadness. She looked in the refrigerator and saw the lasagna she had made for that night's dinner. She took it out. Just a bite, she told herself. She shaved off a small wedge and ate it with her fingers. It felt so good—so comforting. "I shouldn't do this," she said to herself, "this is stupid." But she shaved off another small wedge and ate it. Then another, and another. Pretty soon, she'd eaten two large pieces of lasagna. But she felt so good, better than she had for hours. Her thoughts about Perry had dulled and all she could think about now was being thirsty. "I'll have a small glass of wine, that will help me go to sleep." So she poured herself a glass of wine, and proceeded to eat more lasagna, one sliver at a time.

That first glass of wine was gone and she still didn't feel sleepy. In fact, her angry thoughts about Perry were coming back full force, loosened by the wine. "I can't believe I've put up with him for all these years. Why don't I just tell him off when he's rude to me or Jason? It's because I can't stand conflict. No, it's because I can't think fast enough to come back with a retort. I've always been that way—slow on my feet. That's why I can't seem to make the big money writing software—I can't pitch my ideas convincingly to clients. If they challenge me at all, I crumble and can't come back forcefully. I'm never going to get any interesting projects!"

By 2 A.M., Marina had eaten most of the lasagna and nearly three glasses of wine, at which time her thoughts turned to self-ridicule: "Oh my god, I can't believe I ate all that! How did that happen! I am so full I want to throw up! I'm pathetic, I'm just totally pathetic!" She went to bed in the guest bedroom so as not to wake Perry and proceeded to lie awake for another hour beating up on herself mentally until she finally fell asleep.

Both women and men who are overthinkers are also prone to binge eating and drinking, as well as to depression. But many studies have found that women are more likely than men to fall into the trap of overthinking. When a man faces a distressing situation—say Marina had said something rude to Perry and not vice versa—he tends either to blow it off or confront the situation immediately. Perry might tell himself that Marina must be premenstrual and so forget her remark, or he might come back at her saying, "Boy, you're grumpy, what's wrong with you?" Women are more likely to take the same situation to heart, think about it and analyze it, and go over and over what they should have said or done.

HOW WE GROW OVERTHINKERS

Women aren't just born overthinkers, they are channeled into it by gender roles. In chapter 3, I described the pressures girls and women are under to cope quietly with distress, not impose it on others, but rather manage it within their own bodies and minds. Especially when it comes to anger, women are not allowed to confront or burden others; they are taught from a young age to keep it to themselves and deal with it internally.

I have found in my research that these same social pressures significantly contribute to the development of overthinking in girls and women. For example, women who were most uncomfortable with expressing anger toward others were also most likely to be overthinkers. If you feel unjustified in being angry, or if you feel that you will face the disapproval of others in expressing your anger, you will, like most women, hold it in, letting it stew and grow, and sometimes even seeing it morph into self-hate and despair. Similarly, if you feel no one is interested in helping you deal with situations that make you sad, you'll keep the situation locked inside yourself, going over and over it, trying to figure out some way you can escape.

The social pressure on women to be caregivers to everyone also can contribute to overthinking. I have found that women who are most concerned about keeping everyone happy and about being liked and approved of are highly likely to be overthinkers.[4] Being excessively concerned about relationships leads you to overthink because ambiguity and uncertainty are both rife in relationships, and thus are available to be analyzed to death—an offhand remark by a spouse, an upcoming evaluation from a boss, a coworker who is acting aloof. Women have been taught that it is *their* responsibility to make these situations right, so they spend endless hours replaying exchanges with others, anticipating what others might say, and worrying about the meaning of changes in a relationship. All of this is potent fuel for overthinking.

All-or-Nothing Thinking

Overthinking is even more dangerous to your mental and physical health if you are also prone to engaging in *all-or-nothing thinking*.[5] Without a middle ground, or a gray area, women who engage in this thinking swing from one extreme to the other, their mood and behavior swinging with them.

Jill, whose story we've been following in this book, was well practiced at all-or-nothing thinking. On days when things went well at work, she loved her job and felt extremely competent. A forceful and effective communicator, she pitched new ideas to her clients and could also produce sales materials that were elegantly and creatively written. She could coax extraordinary levels of productivity out of her staff. "I love what I do, and I'm really good at it!" she'd say to herself.

On days that things at work didn't go well, however, Jill's thoughts took a 180-degree turn. If a client seemed bored by her sales pitch, or, heaven forbid, she lost an account, she'd go into a tailspin. She'd repeat in her head again and again the

day's events and the client's remarks. The most negative, ex-
treme perspective would regularly pop into her mind: "I'm
an idiot. I can't put a sentence together. How could I ever
have thought that sales plan would work?" She imagined los-
ing her job, being kicked out of her office without notice,
walking past her staff as they laughed and sneered. "What if
I can't find another job?" she'd wail to herself. "Then I'd
have to move back in with my parents and I'd rather die than
do that!"

It's easy to see how exaggerated negative thoughts can lead to
depression. If you thought you were a complete failure and everyone was against you, you'd feel sad, hopeless, unmotivated. Symptoms of depression occur more often in people who are prone to
all-or-nothing thinking, particularly when they are stressed out or
disappointed. Like Jill, it's difficult to "go with the flow," to recognize that some days are good and some are bad. For some people,
there is no averaging out the days to maintain a balanced sense of
life. Instead, they let their moods be influenced excessively by
whatever happens, feeling either really good or really bad. And
since any day offers something to be frustrated or disappointed
with, all-or-nothing thinkers spend more of their days feeling really bad than feeling really good.

All-or-nothing thinking can also lead to symptoms of eating
and alcohol problems. Several studies have found that women
with significant symptoms of eating disorders are prone to setting
rigid rules and absolute standards for themselves.[6] Just being a
"normal" weight and shape isn't enough—they have to be as

skinny as the models in the magazines or the actresses on TV. It doesn't matter if their body is incapable of being transformed into a semblance of those images because their bone structure or body shape will never allow them to be tall and ultra-thin. They *have* to achieve the skinniest body they possibly can, and they can never be skinny enough.

So they diet. Some women are very successful at dieting. They can deny or ignore symptoms of hunger, even in the face of extreme deprivation and great temptation. These women seem oblivious to their body's signals that it is starving. All they know is that they aren't thin enough yet, so they need to lose more weight. Or, at the very least, not gain any more weight. Women who have these absolute, all-or-nothing attitudes are at special risk for developing symptoms of anorexia nervosa—self-starvation.

Most of us, however, can't deny our body's screams for nourishment. Try as we might, we eat when we are hungry, and we are hungry a lot of the time when we are on a rigid and extreme diet. We may eat a bit, just a little bit, to try to stave off the hunger, only to discover that it's not enough and that we must go back for more. Here's where the all-or-nothing thinking kicks in and sabotages us. We think "I've blown my diet, I might as well blow it all the way." So we eat a lot of the most caloric, fattiest, satisfying foods we can get our hands on. In the scientific literature, this is called the *abstinence violation effect*—we've violated our diet (our abstinence from food) and our all-or-nothing thinking leads us to eat far more than we need to quell our hunger and need for nourishment. Let's return to Jill, whose all-or-nothing thinking often led her to binges such as the one I just described.

The day she lost an important account, Jill went home from work upset and worried. She kept waiting for the phone to ring, and for her boss to tell her he wanted her in his office early the next morning to discuss her failure and incompetence.

She tried to make herself a light, healthy dinner—some soup and a salad—from a menu she had cut out of an article from a women's magazine on losing five pounds in a week. But when she finished eating the allotted portion, she still felt hungry and needy. She decided to have an oatmeal cookie for dessert to make herself feel better, reasoning that at least the oatmeal had some redeeming nutritional value. It tasted really good—until she made the mistake of looking at the label on the package and discovered that just one cookie was 200 calories. She had just gone over the daily quota for calories on this diet by 20 percent!

Now she really felt like a failure. "I can't sell, I can't handle clients, and I can't stay on a simple diet! This is just impossible, the whole thing is impossible. I'll never lose any weight, so why bother?" Jill proceeded to eat the four cookies still left in the package.

The abstinence violation effect also happens with alcohol.[7] All-or-nothing thinking leads women to set up rigid rules about how much they can drink and when. Jill's rules were "I won't drink at all on the weekdays, and I'll never have more than two glasses of wine on weekend nights." If she was good, everything was fine—she felt virtuous and clean and strong. But if she violated the rules, even just a little, she judged herself out of control for lapsing into heavier drinking, as she did the night she lost the account. After Jill ate the five oatmeal cookies, she felt as though all her efforts at self-control were hopeless. The dieting rules had been broken, so why not break the drinking rules, too? Jill opened a magnum of wine and sat down with another box of cookies to drown her thoughts about the horrible day and the consequences that were sure to follow.

The abstinence violation effect doesn't just happen as a result of stress or a traumatic event; it can sneak up in even the most benign circumstances. The only condition needed for the abstinence effect is a rigid set of rules and an all-or-nothing attitude toward them. If you violate the rules and judge yourself harshly, then abandoning all efforts at control is the logical outcome—as Julie, a fifty-year-old homemaker who wanted to reduce her drinking because she had high blood pressure, knows all too well.

Julie read somewhere that alcohol can increase your blood pressure, and she certainly felt her pulse get quicker when she was drinking. She was terrified of hypertension, since her father had died of a heart attack at the age of sixty-five. Julie didn't have other risks for cardiac disease—she was of normal weight and had low cholesterol. Nonetheless, she decided she had to quit drinking altogether in order to lower her risk of heart disease.

This was difficult, since Julie's husband was a food critic for a major metropolitan newspaper and she accompanied him to nice restaurants several nights a week. The meals and wine were paid for by the newspaper so they could afford to eat and drink well. Julie had always loved having a drink with her meals, and hadn't ever had a drinking problem. Her physician had not told her to cut out drinking completely, but Julie nonetheless decided she couldn't let a drop pass her lips.

She kept to this absolute rule for about a month. Then one night when she and her husband were at one of the best restaurants in town, the wine steward recognized them and sent a bottle of extremely expensive fine wine to their table. Julie knew that they would never have ordered such a pricey wine at the paper's expense, or, for that matter, on their own money. She just had to try it. So she allowed the wine steward to pour her a glass. The wine was every bit as good as its reputation. Julie felt a surge of pleasure that she hadn't felt since she'd put herself completely on the wagon.

But her thoughts raced as she sipped. "I'm blowing the rule. This is bad. I'm not supposed to have any wine." These thoughts were met by defiant counter-thoughts: "Who says I can't drink? My doctor never said that. This tastes so good. I would be crazy to pass up this chance." Julie's heart rate increased a bit due to the alcohol and her raging thoughts and she became even more anxious. She just wanted to blank out this anxiety, so she drank more wine and tried to put her attention completely on her husband and the food.

As she ate and talked with her husband, however, she kept lifting the glass to her lips. She was trying so hard to concentrate on anything but the wine and her beating heart and to block out the thoughts in her mind that she didn't notice she

had finished the glass of wine. The steward came by to pour
another glass and she started to wave him off. But she found
herself thinking, "Oh hell, just drink the damn wine," and
gladly accepted another glass.

Julie probably didn't need to worry so much about drinking a little wine at dinner. But her all-or-nothing thinking, as seen in the absolute rule she set for herself, led to the abstinence violation effect—she ended up drinking more than she might have otherwise because, having violated her abstinence, she decided she might as well blow the rule all the way.

All-or-nothing thinking undergirds the toxic triangle by setting up the perfect conditions for all three components simultaneously. When you set absolute rules for yourself that are highly likely to be violated, and then you do in fact violate them, you feel bad about yourself and sink into depression. Then you may eat or drink to escape from that feeling. And if the rules are specifically about how much you can eat or drink, then once they are violated, your all-or-nothing thinking leads not only to depression but also to bingeing on food or alcohol.

Conditions of Self-Esteem

The absolute rules of all-or-nothing thinking can often expand to take the form of "If I do X, then I'll be a good person." Psychologist Jennifer Crocker of the University of Michigan has called these contingencies *conditions of self-esteem*.[8] You set up conditions you (or the world) must meet before you can consider yourself worthy of self-love. As long as you are meeting your conditions, you feel good about yourself. When you aren't meeting them, however, you can feel very bad about yourself.

We all set up conditions for self-esteem—it may be tied to your success at work, or the quality of your family life. Most religions do the same in the form of codes of conduct that should be followed in order to be a good or moral person.

For some of us, however, the conditions we set for our self-esteem are extreme and unattainable. Because of women's roles as caregivers to others, as well as our great empathy for others, many women set up the condition "If everyone loves me, then I'm a good person." They then sacrifice their own needs in order to make this the case. They choose not to confront others in high-conflict situations for fear of being disliked or disapproved of, they go along with unreasonable demands in order to keep others happy, and they overthink interpersonal situations, worrying what other people think and about relationships that aren't going "perfectly."

Not surprisingly, conditions of self-esteem that involve keeping everyone (except perhaps yourself) happy are a setup for disaster. In our research, we found that people who agreed with statements such as "For me to be happy, I need others to be happy" were more likely to be depressed, anxious, and to binge eat when upset. Women were significantly more likely than men to endorse such relationship-oriented conditions of self-esteem.

Societal pressures to be thin offer yet another condition of self-esteem for women who wish to be thin and attractive. If they can achieve this condition, they feel they are in control, strong, and superior. If they can't achieve it, they are a failure, bad, or unlovable. Jennifer Crocker has found that women who set up appearance-related conditions of self-esteem are more vulnerable to depression and to symptoms of eating disorders.[9] They become depressed when they fail to meet their standards for loving themselves, while the symptoms of eating disorders arise when they either starve themselves to meet their conditions of self-esteem or fall into the abstinence violation effect when they fail to do so.

Silvie, a twenty-two-year-old mother of young twin boys, lived in constant fear of slipping from her standard of being extremely thin. The first thing you noticed about Silvie was her arms. They were like sticks. Her bones stuck out and there seemed to be no flesh. The rest of her body was nearly devoid of fat, and her clothes often hung on her.

The first thing Silvie did every morning was weigh herself. Her goal was to remain at 105 pounds, well under the "healthy" weight for her 5-foot, 6-inch frame. If she went over 105 by even a pound, she would cut back on her eating until she got back to 105. If she went under 105, she felt as if she had some "wiggle room" in her diet and could eat a bit more that day, although subconsciously she was gleeful about weighing even less than 105.

Silvie was aware of every morsel that went into her mouth. She didn't really count calories, but she knew exactly how much she ate in a typical day, and if she exceeded her usual amount, she would become moderately panicked. She would go back over what she had eaten at every meal and snack, analyzing any situation that had led her to eat more than she was "allowed." She would then vow to avoid that situation in the future. As long as she kept rigid control over her weight, Silvie felt good about herself. She loved being so thin, although she was annoyed when people expressed concern about her weight.

Occasionally, because of bloating when she was premenstrual, or because she actually ate more than usual, Silvie's weight would increase by a few pounds. If she stepped on the scale in the morning and it read 108, or even 110, her heart sank. She felt ugly and fat. Her mind raced as she tried to determine the source of her added weight. If it was due to the meal she had the night before, she would chastise herself for "pigging out." If she couldn't determine why she had gained weight, she began to worry that she wouldn't be able to control her weight in the future. Regardless of the reason, she felt horrible about herself. She ate as little as she could the rest of the day, and prayed that her weight would be back to normal by the next morning.

Silvie's standards for her weight, and for her behavior more generally, were extreme, but many women have a similar mindset. On "skinny days" we feel good about ourselves. On "heavy days" we don't.

The combination of appearance-related conditions of self-esteem and all-or-nothing thinking sets up women for at least two components of the toxic triangle. Psychologist Kathleen Vohs of Case Western Reserve University in Ohio and her colleagues found that women who had both rigid, perfectionist beliefs and felt they weren't meeting the personal standards for their weight set by those beliefs were especially likely to have symptoms of depression and bulimia.[10]

Basing your self-worth on appearance may also lead to heavy drinking. In studies of high school and college students, Jennifer Crocker found that students with appearance-related conditions of self-esteem drank more heavily in their first year of college than students who didn't.[11] Crocker speculates that this may be because students who were concerned with their appearance were more likely to join groups that focused on appearance and social status, such as sororities, which in turn exposed them to more peer pressure to drink.

Crocker also finds that basing self-worth on any type of external condition dependent on the opinions of others puts women at risk for depression and maladaptive ways of coping with stress.[12] When your opinion of yourself depends on meeting external standards, you are at the mercy of others' judgments and attitudes toward you. Other people are, as we know, not always generous, so there is always room to worry about what others think, making your self-esteem highly unstable, which in turn sets you up for depression and unhealthy behaviors such as binge eating or drinking.

Unfortunately, women are more likely than men to have external conditions of self-esteem, particularly those related to appearance or how well they are liked by others. Again, this is probably because we women have spent our lives being encouraged to care what others think of us and to look good by society's standards. These external conditions of self-esteem, however, are yet another factor that influences the toxic triangle.

Some Good News!

The same brain that overthinks and sets us up with unreasonable expectations for ourselves can also be trained to defeat these self-destructive tendencies, even in those women who have a biological vulnerability to fall into the toxic triangle. Research shows a variety of strategies that can help women overcome unhealthy attitudes and regain control over their lives. We can implement these strategies for ourselves, and they are the focus of chapter 6.

SIX

=▼=

Transforming Vulnerabilities
into Strengths

J UST THINKING ABOUT the social, psychological, and biological forces pushing women toward the toxic triangle may be
enough to make you depressed, want to drink, or binge eat! Indeed, most women find themselves some distance down the road
to the toxic triangle over the course of their lives. So now it is
time for the good news for women, and for the people who love
them and want to help them.

We can transform our vulnerabilities into strengths because
we have the tools to change the way we cope with stressful circumstances. Be it exploitative relationships or the expectations of
others—these stresses don't need to damage our bodies and send
us into the toxic triangle. Each of us can change the ways we
think about ourselves, so that instead of living our lives to please
other people, we live them to the fullest.

Women are good at self-focused coping because we are highly attuned to our own emotions and the emotions of others. The rich emotional lives that women enjoy include thinking about our feelings, talking about them with others, and caring about other people's feelings, but these abilities can also get us into trouble. When our emotional sensitivities and tendencies to contemplate go too far, we fall into overthinking and can become overwhelmed by our own emotions. Excessively concerned about our relationships, we can behave in ways that suit others' best interests rather than our own.

But we can turn our emotional sensitivities, ability to think deeply, and empathy for others on their heads and use them to our advantage. We can use our self-awareness to recognize and tolerate our problems and our painful emotions rather than running away from them through overeating or drinking. We can use our empathy for others to accept their faults, understand them, and influence our relationships. We can also use our concern for others as a motivator for our own positive change.

We need tools, however, to harness the good energy of our reflective and interpersonal skills, so that we can counter our tendency to self-focus or to be more concerned for others than we are for ourselves—both entry points into the toxic triangle. These tools break down into two categories. One category is those that allow us to step back from our thoughts and concerns, take stock of them, and realize how they are affecting our behavior. In this chapter, I will describe how these tools work, showing you how they can help you break free of troubling thoughts and unhealthy goals that rule you and drive you into depression, yo-yo eating, and heavy drinking.

The other category of tools, which I will detail in chapter 7, involves strategies to make choices about how we want to think about our world and ourselves. These will enable us to take positive action to carry out those choices and inoculate ourselves against the toxic triangle.

The Master and the Slave

If our sensitivities to our own emotions and the emotions of others, and our ability to think deeply about ourselves and others, are such assets, how do they drag us into the toxic triangle? This happens when our emotions and our concerns about others take on a life of their own and begin to rule us like a master rules a slave. We may talk about "my feelings" and "my worries about others," but we really treat them as if they are a living, breathing demon that has seized control of our minds and bodies. When this demon demands our attention, we are compelled to give in to it, letting ourselves be consumed by the feelings and concerns it commands from us. We may feel overwhelmed and miserable, but still we attend to this demon because it is our master. We cannot ignore or dispute it, because it—not us—is in command.

Our behaviors, as well as our thoughts, can become slaves to our feelings. If we are consumed by sadness or regret, we shut down and close up, fully believing the horrible things our feelings are saying to us—that we are no good, that no one loves us, that everything is hopeless—because they are the master, and so must be right. We may try to escape, at least for a short time, by binge eating or drinking. But then the master has that much more to berate us for: "You weakling, you know you can control your drinking!" "You're going to be fat as a pig eating like that!" We accept these thoughts as true and real. We *should* feel guilty and ashamed. We violated the rules that say you have to be completely in control, thin, and perfect in the eyes of others. We accept our punishment—self-loathing and despair—and redouble our efforts to follow the rules completely . . . until the next time we are driven to escape their tyranny by absorbing ourselves in drinking or eating.

The First Step to Freedom

The first step to freedom is to realize that the master is not real. It is a false god like those of ancient times. It is no more real than the statues that ancient peoples erected to portray those gods. The master exists only in our minds and so only we have the power to keep it alive.

Now, this doesn't mean that the master has no force over us. Just as ancient peoples would sacrifice their lives for false gods, many women sacrifice their lives obeying the commands of their negative emotions and thoughts. They suffer the self-destruction of depression, they drink alcohol until their bodies disintegrate, they let their weight be the defining feature of who they are, they make decisions that are driven by what they think other people want of them.

But our false gods are no less an illusion. Once they are recognized for what they are, dismissed, or torn down, we can replace them with values and goals that we actively choose. Let me make this more concrete with the story of Anna, a thirty-seven-year-old homemaker who has been plagued by the toxic triangle since adolescence.

Anna is a woman ruled by "shoulds":

"I should keep my house cleaner."

"I should let my elderly parents move in with us."

"I should be more active in my church."

Anna's "should" obsessions came in part from her relationship with her mother. Anna is of Italian descent, short, dark-skinned, and a fabulous cook. She loves whipping up elaborate Italian meals for her family, and they love eating them. But everyone in her family, including Anna, is quite a bit overweight. Still, when her parents were at Anna's house for dinner, her mother scolded Anna for cooking too little food: "You're trying to starve us!" So the next time around, when Anna was cooking for the extended family, she heard her mother's voice in her ear, and cooked up much more than she knew her family would eat, or baked a rich, fattening dessert, in case anyone could eat more after the main courses were done.

One day, when Anna had been cooking for hours in preparation for a big family dinner, her daughter, Sophie, walked in and asked, "Ma, why do you cook so much? We can't eat all that. We don't want to eat all that!"

Anna replied, "Because I have to. It's the way it's done. My family shouldn't go hungry."

"But Ma, we never go hungry! Just 'cause Grandma says we should all eat like pigs doesn't mean we have to! I don't want Daddy to have a heart attack at the age of sixty, like Uncle Frank. I don't want to have to starve myself all day long, like you do, so I can eat enough at dinnertime to please Grandma! Sheesh, Ma, get a life!"

Sophie had a tendency to be opinionated, so Anna was accustomed to her outbursts. But this one really caught her attention. Was she doing something she shouldn't by cooking fancy meals for her family? But her mother said she should cook more. What should she be doing?

Then Sophie's demand that she "get a life" rang in Anna's head. Was Anna letting her mother, and other people, rule her life and make demands on her? What did she think was the right thing to do?

Anna set her knife down on her chopping board and sat on one of the stools at the kitchen island. She looked around the kitchen and first saw the cannolis she had made earlier in the day—fancy cream-filled Italian pastries that were a zillion calories each. She was surprised to hear her mother's voice in her head saying, "You made them too small! They are barely one bite each for the men! You should have made them bigger, and sprinkled them with powdered sugar! Didn't I teach you anything?"

Then she looked further around the kitchen and saw the television. She remembered earlier in the day watching a program in which a physician was talking about the rise in obesity in the United States and how it was leading to a dramatic increase in diabetes and stroke. An image of her husband, Giuseppe, eating a cannoli and then keeling over in his chair with a stroke flashed into her mind. In this image, Sophie ran up and yelled, "You killed him, Ma, you killed him!"

Anna put her head in her hands and started to weep. She was so tired. Tired of trying to please her mother. Tired of trying to do "what's right." Who knew what was right—her mother? The physician on TV? Sophie? All three of their voices echoed in her head, making her dizzy.

So Anna lifted her head, and as if speaking directly to the voices, said out loud, "I know what's right. Keeping my family healthy is right. I love them too much to put them in their grave to please my mother."

Anna walked over to the cannolis, picked up the tray, opened the lid on the trash can, and dumped them in. Then she picked up the phone and dialed her mother. "Ma," she said, "I can't cook dinner tonight. I'm sorry for such short notice, but you and Dad are going to have to eat on your own." Before her mother could argue with her, Anna said she had to go, and hung up the phone. Then she picked up her jacket, walked out the door, and took a walk through the neighborhood to clear her head and think about how she wanted to take care of her family.

Anna had the critical benefit of Sophie's outburst to help her recognize that she was letting her mother's demands on her, and other "shoulds," rule her behaviors and attitudes. Many of us don't have family members or friends who are as perceptive as Sophie is in identifying our demons or who are brave enough to confront us with them. Indeed, for many of us, our problems lie in the relationships we have with others and the ways we let those relationships dictate how we feel about ourselves and how we behave.

So What Do We Do Instead?

Scientists have developed several different strategies for identifying the kinds of thoughts and feelings that contribute to symptoms of depression or anxiety, the tendency to overeat, or periods of binge drinking. These strategies are crucial first steps in the journey out of the toxic triangle and back to health and well-being. Some of these strategies will appeal to you more than others; try several of them and discover which ones fit your style. All of these strategies will help you identify the thoughts that run through your head—often without you consciously being aware of them—in times when you are feeling down or upset, or when you want to binge eat or drink.

Most negative thoughts are likely to share some core themes, which will probably be connected to the internal and external pressures on women we talked about in chapters 3 and 5. You may quickly recognize the themes reflecting the social pressures to be thin: "Everything would be okay if I could just lose a few more pounds." Or "My weight is my biggest problem." You may recognize themes that reflect the pressure for women to be excessively concerned about their relationships, in thoughts such as "I couldn't live if he fell out of love with me." Or "I can't stand it if someone doesn't like me." Look also for signs of all-or-nothing thinking: "If I can't lose all twenty pounds, I might as well give up!" Or "If I'm not completely abstinent, then I'm a drunk." And listen for your own personal conditions of self-esteem in statements such as "In order to feel good about myself, I must . . ."

These are painful things to hear yourself saying, but the critical first step to a more fulfilling life is to identify your false gods and recognize how they are dragging you down emotionally and driving your unhealthy behaviors. It's not always easy to hear or recognize the voices of our internal demons. Mindfulness techniques can be invaluable in quieting the din in our heads so we can tune in to these voices.

Mindfulness

Mindfulness techniques are a set of tools that are taking the field of psychology by storm. Although these specific tools are new to psychology, they are actually very old; they come from meditation practices developed by practitioners of Eastern philosophies and religions such as Buddhism. If you've taken yoga classes, or read any of the several popular books on meditation, you've been introduced to them.

Though it may sound a bit mystical, modern hard science is showing that meditation can be extremely helpful to people who are plagued by negative thoughts and feelings and out-of-control behaviors. Research has shown that mindfulness training can help people who have a long history of serious depression avoid future episodes.[1] Other research has successfully used mindfulness techniques to help people who are addicted to alcohol or who binge eat gain control over their impulsive bingeing.[2]

In one study, people addicted to alcohol or drugs learned mindfulness techniques and found that they helped them control their alcohol and drug use and reduce their symptoms of anxiety and depression. In addition, those who learned mindfulness techniques were more optimistic about their future, were better able to cope with negative emotions and urges, and were more ready to make other positive changes in their lives.[3]

One of the things I like about mindfulness techniques is that they capitalize on the emotional and contemplative strengths of women. Mindfulness basically involves expanding our awareness of our internal thoughts and feelings, focusing our attention on the present moment, and becoming aware of our habitual patterns of responding to stressful circumstances.

But unlike the kind of ruminative overthinking that some of us fall into, mindfulness involves acknowledging these thoughts and feelings without judging or trying to get rid of them. One characteristic of overthinking is the sense of being in a hyperevaluative mode, analyzing every emotion we have: "What's wrong with me that I'm feeling sad?" "I'm going to fall apart if I can't stop feeling anxious!" We question our every thought and motive, and everything other people say: "How could he have said that to me?" "What does it mean that I'm not excited about this vacation?" And then we apply our rigid, perfectionistic rules for being a "good person" in order to judge ourselves as being out of control or a failure: "I'm such a loser because I haven't lost weight (or been able to stop drinking)." "I should feel bad about myself because my angry outburst hurt someone else's feelings!" These thoughts and feelings are so compelling that we believe they must be true—why else would we be having them if they weren't?

Mindfulness teaches us to notice our thoughts, feelings, bodily sensations, and memories without immediately categorizing them as good or bad. We learn to be more compassionate toward ourselves, responding to our thoughts and feelings as a friend might, rather than as a slave to a master. By being able to step back and notice, rather than be overwhelmed or ruled by our feelings, we become better able to choose how we want to feel and act in difficult situations.

So that you can get a sense of what this practice is like, let's try a mindfulness exercise developed by psychologists Zindel Segal, Mark Williams, and John Teasdale.[4] Do this exercise in a quiet room, alone, sitting in a comfortable chair.

❖ First, close your eyes and focus on your breathing for a couple of minutes. Notice how your breath travels into your body, through your body, and back out of your body. Notice what parts of your body move as you breathe.

Next, tune in to the thoughts that are going through your mind, much as you might to a radio playing in the background. Try to let the thoughts flow by, noting them, but not latching on to any one of them. It's okay if they are critical (such as "This is a dumb exercise" or "How could this possibly help?"). If that's what's going through your mind, then that's how it is. Just let yourself say, "Okay, that's what I'm thinking right now."

Note the way your body feels right now. Is there any sense of tension or discomfort? Rather than try to push these feelings away, acknowledge them, saying, "Okay, that's how I'm feeling right now." If you start to feel pulled in by your feelings or thoughts, imagine yourself as a trusted friend to them, acknowledging them compassionately, but staying outside and observing them.

You are now aware of what's going on in your mind right at the moment. Now, turn your attention back to your breathing. Focus on the movements of your abdomen, the rise and fall of your breath. Spend a minute or two focusing on each breath as it moves in and out. Use your awareness of your breath to be completely present in the moment.

Now let your awareness expand to your whole body. Get a sense of your body as a whole, including any feelings of tenseness or fatigue. Follow your breath in and out as if your whole body was breathing. Notice your more spacious awareness of your whole body.

Then, when you are ready, allow your eyes to open.

What did you notice about yourself while you were doing this exercise? As you were doing it, was it difficult not to get caught up in your thoughts or feelings? This is very common when you first practice mindfulness. The habit of being consumed by certain negative thoughts and feelings is an old one that is strongly ingrained and takes some time to break. Also, mindfulness is a process. You don't do it a right or a wrong way—you continually bring yourself back to a mindful stance each time thoughts and feelings pull you into negative territory.

One mindfulness technique specially designed for people who have cravings or urges to binge on alcohol or food is called *urge surfing*.[5] Urges behave like waves—they start small, build to a crest, then break up and dissolve. When you urge surf, you ride the wave rather than fighting it; as a result, you are less likely to be pulled in and/or wiped out.

❖ There are three basic steps to urge surfing:

1. When you first notice a craving, sit in a comfortable chair with your feet flat on the floor and your hands in a comfortable position. Take a few deep breaths and focus your attention on your body. Notice where in your body you are experiencing the craving. For each area of your body that senses a craving, describe what it is like. For example, you might say, "I feel it in my stomach, it is like a gnawing." Or "My mouth feels like it desperately wants a certain taste."

2. Focus on one area in which you are experiencing the urge and notice exactly what you are sensing there. Are your muscles tense or relaxed? Is the area large, like an aching feeling all over your abdomen, or is it small? Track the changes that occur in the sensations: "At first I barely noticed a longing feeling in my bones, but now I feel it intensely."

3. Repeat the process of intense focus on each of the areas of your body in which you are experiencing the urge, noticing how it ebbs and flows. Many people notice that after a few minutes, the urge subsides considerably. But if this doesn't happen, just continue to ride it, noticing how it moves and changes, until it does diminish.

Let's try another exercise, this one called *Leaves Flowing in a Stream*.[6] The purpose of this exercise is to see how quickly thoughts can pull us away from our experience of the moment. What I want you to do is to think whatever thoughts come to mind, and allow them to flow, one after another. Notice when there is a shift from looking *at* your thoughts to looking from *inside* your thoughts.

❖ First, get comfortable, close your eyes, and spend a couple of minutes noticing your breath going in and out. Now, imagine that there are a bunch of leaves gathered by the bank of a peaceful, flowing stream. You are standing on the bank of the stream, watching as the current pulls the leaves gently down the stream. As the leaves flow by, let each thought you are having rest on the center of a leaf. If you have a hard time putting your thoughts into words, see the thoughts as images, and place each image in the center of a leaf.

Watch the leaves go by, your thoughts upon them, flowing along. At some point, you are likely to have the sense that the leaves have stopped flowing, or that you are in a stream with the leaves instead of on the bank watching them float by, or you might have lost the image of the stream altogether. When this happens, pause for a few seconds and notice what was going on right before the leaves stopped flowing. What thoughts were going through your mind? What might have distracted you? What feelings were you having? Did you want to stop the exercise?

Now go ahead and let your stream of thoughts, each on a leaf, start flowing again. And notice again when the flow stops or the image is lost, and see if you can catch what was happening this time. If you begin to tell yourself, "I can't do this," or "I'm not doing this right," or "This isn't working," put *those* thoughts on a leaf and let them flow down the stream. After a few minutes, open your eyes and gently let go of the exercise.

People have lots of different reactions to exercises like the three just described. Some find them really hard to do. If that is your experience, it might be helpful to get a book that is devoted to helping you learn mindfulness exercises, such as Jon Kabat-Zinn's *Wherever You Go, There You Are: Mindfulness Meditation in Everyday Life,* or perhaps consider joining a class that teaches meditation techniques.

The point of mindfulness exercises is to give you tools to step back from your thoughts and feelings and break free of the grip they have on your mind and your body. Often you are not even aware that certain thoughts and feelings are flowing through you, but nevertheless they have a major effect on your body and your behaviors, dragging you down into the symptoms of depression and anxiety or motivating you to escape through binge eating or drinking. At other times, hyper-aware of them, you believe there is nothing you can do to stop them, and so you let yourself be consumed.

Mindfulness exercises teach you to tune in to those thoughts and feelings, which is different from accepting their rule over you. By taking an observer's perspective, watching them float by, not judging or evaluating them, not panicking because you have them, you understand that your thoughts and feelings are something that happens in you, but *they are not you*. You are an individual who can stand apart from these thoughts and feelings. You can observe them and recognize their effect on you. Then you can decide which ones you want to have and which ones you don't.

If you find it difficult to take this observer stance, try this technique, which capitalizes on your ability as a woman to empathize with others.

❖ Imagine that your own thoughts and feelings are not yours but belong to a close friend, someone you really care about. Imagine that she is telling you about them. You are listening intently, as a close friend does, but not saying anything—you are giving her the space to voice her concerns without giving any advice or feedback. You are just trying to hear what she has to say, compassionately, knowing that these are her concerns and not necessarily your own. Are there certain themes in what she says? Does anything alarm you? Can you understand why she feels the way she does? Are there different ways she might think about her problems?

Mindfulness techniques also teach you to be more aware of the present moment. Most of us spend much of our time embroiled in rehashing things that have happened in the past, or thinking about what might happen in the future. As a result, we are not very aware of what is going on right in front of our faces—our child's smile, our boss's frown, the tension in our own bodies. Our unhealthy and compulsive behaviors—like binge drinking and overeating—can serve as methods to escape the cacophony of thoughts, memories, and worries in our minds. Mindfulness practice helps us be more centered in the present so that we can appreciate the good things that reside there and, in contrast, recognize the people and situations that are triggering negative emotions and thoughts. By practicing "being with" our feelings and thoughts, we can become less frightened and overwhelmed by them, and thus less motivated to escape them with unhealthy behaviors. We can also learn a great deal about ourselves, particularly the ways we have internalized social pressures to cast ourselves in a certain light (for example, in terms of how much we weigh) or to behave in certain ways (such as always putting others' needs before our own).

Jill, the woman we have been following throughout this book, didn't realize until she joined a yoga class the extent to which her feelings about herself and her unhealthy eating and drinking were driven by concerns about how attractive she was. She was reluctant to join the class, but her friend Katie coaxed her into it. Jill was relieved when she saw that the flyer for the class said to come in loose baggy clothes, because she had imagined that class members were expected to wear those skimpy leotards that many women at health clubs wear, and the idea of anyone seeing her in such an outfit filled her with horror. She wasn't really overweight—her self-starvation during the week more or less compensated for her binge eating on the weekend. But she felt dumpy and unattractive and avoided any situation in which other people would see her shape up close.

At first Jill found the class difficult. She wasn't limber and she felt uncomfortable focusing on her body. But she enjoyed the breathing exercises and found herself much less tense after each class.

Jill started practicing yoga at home between classes and began to recognize how much more positive she felt about her body—as if she had gained a sense of ownership and the beginning of satisfaction, even pride, in it. This contrasted sharply with the sense of alienation she'd had before she began yoga.

Jill hadn't been happy with how she looked since she went through puberty earlier than her girlfriends in fifth grade and gained a lot of weight. She felt big and lumpy and uncoordinated compared to the other girls. And, as we noted earlier, Jill's father added to her concerns by teasing her and calling her "tub butt." Jill didn't date much in high school, and she attributed this to being heavier and less pretty than the other girls. Actually, it probably had more to do with the fact that Jill was extremely smart and the boys were intimidated by her.

As an adult, Jill attended a prestigious college and landed a job in the marketing division of a large company, where she excelled and quickly rose through the ranks. Now she was an executive vice president, in charge of the company's western U.S. division and responsible for millions of dollars in business per year. Jill felt good about her accomplishments, but still, her sense of being unattractive diminished her self-esteem. She felt lonely and sad, and she continued to turn to drinking and binge eating to smother these feelings.

The more she practiced yoga and developed her ability to tune in to her own body, as well as her feelings about it, the more Jill recognized the extent to which she had accepted some unreasonable standard for how she should look. She was somewhat angry with herself for buying into that standard and letting it affect her self-esteem and social life so much.

Like Jill, we may berate ourselves when we recognize the kinds of negative thoughts or expectations we have of ourselves, or the unhealthy ways we try to escape from these thoughts. "I'm so stupid to let other people determine how I feel! I'm so weak to use alcohol to cover up my feelings! I'm pathetic for binge eating when I'm feeling upset!" As we practice mindfulness, it is critical to maintain a compassionate stance vis-à-vis ourselves. After all, we are simply trying to understand what thoughts and feelings are troubling us. We are not there to judge them or even to try to control them. Just as a trusted friend would listen compassionately to our deepest secrets and not think less of us for revealing them, we must listen with trust to our own deepest secrets and respond with love.

Women can be extremely good at doing this. But all of us have periods in which we lose track of what we really think or feel. We become so caught up in taking care of others that we don't take care of ourselves, either by not listening to our body's signals that our behavior is unhealthy or by ignoring our own values and desires in favor of pleasing other people. We let the norms of society define who we should be, rather than allowing us to conceive our own definitions. When we are on autopilot, doing and feeling but not noticing, we are especially likely to engage in unhealthy behaviors like overeating or drinking—mindless, compulsive behaviors.[7]

That's when we need to actively practice being mindful—listening to the self we've lost track of, and being gentle and loving toward that self: "No wonder you are stressed. No wonder you want to escape. So that's what you're feeling. . . ." Mindfulness makes you aware of the triggers that cause your craving. In addition, it allows you to identify the craving, accept that it is there, but step back from it instead of mindlessly acting on it. The more you practice a mindful response to your cravings and urges to binge, the more you will feel a sense of strength rather than powerlessness.

You may protest that you are painfully aware of your negative feelings and thoughts—that's the problem after all! It's certainly true that women who suffer from depression and anxiety are chronically aware of their symptoms of sadness or tension, as well as their worries or regrets. Women don't usually take a mindful stance toward these symptoms, instead they feel consumed and overwhelmed by a litany of their complaints about themselves. The toxic triangle offers a false escape for them.

Mindfulness can teach us to be neither consumed by our feelings and thoughts nor ready to escape them through unhealthy behaviors. Instead we become aware of them in a way that breaks their grip on us and frees us to make better choices for ourselves.

The Diary Method

If mindfulness techniques don't appeal to you, an alternative that I call the *Diary Method* also taps women's self-reflective strengths. This method can be used in conjunction with mindfulness techniques as well.

The goal of the Diary Method is to keep an ongoing, written record of key events in your day and how you think and feel about them. By a key event, I mean any situation in which you find yourself having a significant urge to drink or binge eat, or one in which you feel yourself becoming blue, depressed, or anxious. There may be something specific that triggers these urges and feelings—a difficult interaction with another person, going by a restaurant, being alone at home. Or they may come from out of the blue. It doesn't matter, just write down what is going on, and then get quiet for a moment and tune in to what is going through your head. What kinds of thoughts are you having? "I want a drink so badly!" "I'm just starved, I need to eat!" "It's all hopeless, just hopeless!" Write down your feelings. Are they a mix of longing, anxiety, sadness, defeat? Does one feeling predominate? What's happening around you? Who is there? What have they said to you? What have you said to them?

Instead of waiting until the end of the day to reflect on it, it's best to keep this diary nearby and record key events as they occur so that you can tune in to your thoughts and feelings as they are happening, recording them accurately in your diary. This is the first step toward becoming aware of their presence in your life. If you wait until the end of the day, you may not remember some of your thoughts, or they may morph and change over the course of the day. That morphing and changing is interesting, too, and can be recorded later in the day. The specific thoughts and feelings that you capture as they unfold will help you begin to recognize the way in which they conspire to lead you into symptoms of the toxic triangle. Let's meet Peggy, a thirty-two-year-old freelance writer, who uses the Diary Method to understand themes in her thoughts and how they lead her to drink and feel sad.

Peggy had spent the day working in her home office, but it hadn't been pleasant. She had experienced an old-fashioned writer's block most of the day, and by the time her husband, Lyle, came home, she was frustrated, tired, and disgusted with herself. As he did most nights, her husband poured himself a drink shortly after he got into the house. He asked Peggy if he could pour her one.

In the old days, Peggy would have always said yes, but she decided a few weeks ago that she wanted to cut back on her drinking. She had gained about ten pounds over the last year, and knew that when she drank, she tended to overeat. Plus, there were a lot of calories in the alcohol itself, so she thought cutting down on drinking would help her lose weight in a couple of ways. It was clear that the day after she drank quite a bit, she would be fatigued and have trouble concentrating, and she was concerned that this was reducing her productivity at writing.

Peggy had told Lyle that she wanted to cut back on her drinking, so she was annoyed at him when he asked her if he could make her a drink. On the other hand, the idea of a drink after such a frustrating day was so inviting!

Rather than answer Lyle's question immediately, Peggy went into the bedroom to get some privacy. She sat on the bed, got quiet, and breathed in deeply for a couple of minutes. Then she tuned in to her thoughts. She heard herself saying, "I deserve this drink. I need this drink. I've been drinking for years and still writing. Why do I think I need to stop? Things go so much better with Lyle if we are both relaxing with a drink. He gets nervous when I don't drink— thinks I'm changing the rules or something."

Several important themes arise in Peggy's thoughts, one of which is self-medication. She has been using alcohol to cope with feelings of frustration and questions about her competence as a writer for years, and to some extent she still believes she can get away with this. Another theme has to do with the role of alcohol in her marriage. Alcohol "smoothes the way" in her interactions with her husband, and it seems as if both Peggy and Lyle need to relax with alcohol in order to have a good conversation with each other. Also, her husband is putting pressure on her to drink, perhaps because if she abstains it raises questions in his own mind about why he needs to drink every night.

Research on drinking has shown that there are some common triggers for binges.[8] With the benefit of a few days of diary entries, some themes may become evident:

1. Particular individuals are usually involved in the situation, and they are often drinking themselves.

2. There are certain places where you have drunk too much in the past, and certain places you find it hard not to drink in the present, such as parties or bars, after work at home, weekends.

3. You drink when you have certain emotions, such as frustration, fear, fatigue, stress, or tension. You drink in response to positive emotions, such as being excited or having feelings of accomplishment.

4. You have an urge to drink, and say to yourself things like, "I can't stand this. This urge is going to get stronger until I blow up or drink something."

Some of these same triggers apply to binge eating, which tends to begin in certain places or in response to certain emotions.[9] A major trigger for binge eating is excessive dieting.[10] We let ourselves get so hungry before we will eat anything that our bodies are screaming for fast calories; when we finally do eat something, we eat too quickly and go for high-calorie foods, where binges tend to be born.

It is likely that you may begin to recognize the theme of relationships or a certain relationship in your diary accounts. It may be your relationship with your spouse that often seems to be a trigger for negative feelings or unhealthy behaviors. It may be relationships with people in your workplace—you find yourself trying to "manage" everyone's feelings or worry excessively about how they feel about you. There may be certain friends you tend to be with when you lapse into drinking too much. As you begin to recognize the role of key people in these difficult times, use your reflective abilities to consider what it is about them that contributes to your sad or anxious feelings, or to your desire to drink or eat. How do they make you feel about yourself? What kinds of pressures might they be putting on you—subtly or not—to behave in ways you later regret?

When you are binge drinking or eating, another question to ask yourself is "What is this behavior doing for me?" or "What am I getting out of this?" You keep engaging in bingeing, even when you believe you should stop, because drinking and eating are reinforcing—they are giving you something positive that you keep coming back for. Yes, they may feel good, at least in the short term. Eating and alcohol can also buy us rewards, even if we aren't aware we're getting them. They can buy us escape from nagging concerns about our self-worth or our relationships, for instance, or excuses for avoiding situations we are uncomfortable with, like going to work the next day. Alcohol can, as in Peggy's case, smooth over problems in a relationship. And alcohol or eating can become a part of our identity—"I like drinking a lot, that's just who I am." Or "I am addicted to food."

Your diary entries don't all have to be about negative situations. It's also important to recognize those situations and people that make you feel good, or make it easier to control your eating or your drinking. If you spend an evening with a friend and don't even think about drinking or eating, write about this in your diary when you get home. What is it about that friend that makes you able to enjoy yourself without going overboard? How does this friend make you feel—valued and appreciated, listened to, intellectually invigorated? Were you in some place that helped you curb your urges? For example, perhaps you were in a restaurant where the food was so good you wanted to savor every bite rather than gobble down as much as you could. Positive situations such as these give you lots of information that you can use to develop new strategies for making yourself happier and taking better care of your body.

What Do I Do Now?

You've already taken the major step of learning ways to observe your habitual thoughts, feelings, and behaviors, and to identify their major themes and triggers. At this point, you may be thinking, "What do I do now? I can't change all these things about my life and how I think and feel! It's too much! I have no control!" It is this very sense of being overwhelmed and having no control that leads many women to step off the path that takes them into health, and move back onto the path that leads into the toxic triangle. Most women get to this crossroads at some point on their journey to well-being; some women must face the crossroads many times.

It is at this juncture that you should further call upon your interpersonal strengths as a woman for help. If you have someone in your life you trust and believe has your best interests at heart, consider confiding in this person about the themes and issues you've identified in your mindfulness or diary practices. Your goal or expectation shouldn't be for this person to "fix" your problems. Rather, by sharing what you've discovered about yourself with someone who can validate your concerns, you may find out that she has been concerned about you as well. Enlist this person to accompany you as you begin to make positive changes in your life. Committing to changes with, or in front of, another person can greatly increase the odds that you'll stick with the changes when the going gets tough. If you don't have a friend or family member who fits the bill, you might consult someone you respect—a clergyperson, a professional counselor, or a self-help group.

Yet another way you can use your interpersonal strengths to move forward is to think about important people in your life for whom you want to change. Many women who spend time battling the toxic triangle say that they would rather be using that time in positive interactions with their children. Others want to be a better role model or caregiver to their children. Either of these goals can give women tremendous motivation and strength to make changes.

Your strengths at self-reflection can also be used to respond to feelings of "I can't deal with this!" When you find yourself veering off the path to health, try this mini-mindfulness technique.

❖ Sit down, get quiet, shut your eyes, and let your thoughts and feelings flow. Step back from them and watch where they go. What do you notice? If you just observe them, do they grow bigger and bigger? Do they jump around from one concern to another? Or do they eventually fade out? How does your body feel? Tense? Weighed down? Full of urges to bolt and go eat or drink? What happens if you just ride those urges for a few minutes?

Try to respond to yourself with acceptance and compassion: "So that's what I'm feeling. Okay, there's where that thought is going. Hmm, there's a lot in there." Try to be the caring and wise friend you need right now, hearing your own thoughts and feelings nonjudgmentally. After a few minutes, slowly open your eyes.

You've just spent several minutes with thoughts and feelings of being overwhelmed and out of control. But they didn't consume you. You didn't get up and run to the refrigerator or liquor cabinet. And perhaps those thoughts seem a bit different to you now—a little more distant, less a part of you and more just "out there."

You have come a long way. You have learned how to use your self-reflective powers to discover some of the forces pushing you into the toxic triangle. You have developed some strategies for getting back on the path to health when the traveling gets difficult. The next major step is to choose your new destination— where you want to be in your life—and then to begin to move toward that home, equipped with the tools you need to get you there.

SEVEN

Moving toward a Healthier You

IF YOU'RE NOT going to live your life by the rules imposed on you by society—the rules that say we have to cope on our own and not bother other people, that we must consider others' feelings before our own, that we must look a certain way; in short, that we have to base our self-worth on standards set by other people—then what standards *are* you going to use?

The odds are high that if you've read this far, one of your life goals is to escape the toxic triangle: "I want to stop drinking." "I want to stop overeating." "I want to stop being depressed all the time." Or you may say, "I want to stop being concerned with how I look." Or "I want to stop sacrificing my own needs for other people." Or "I want to stop being so hard on myself." Some readers may be concerned about a family member or friend who seems to be suffering from symptoms of the toxic triangle.

These are good goals, but research on motivational processes has shown that it's difficult to accomplish goals that are defined as avoiding something or getting rid of something about yourself. Instead, it is easier to accomplish *approach goals,* which move you toward a positive change.[1] In this chapter, I will teach you how to use your powers of self-reflection to decide which goals you want to approach—the changes you want to make and how you want to live your life—and design strategies to get you to that place. The exercises you learned in chapter 6 made you aware of what you want to leave behind—toxic thoughts, feelings, and behaviors that suck the life out of you. The exercises in this chapter move you yet further forward, into a new place where you can be healthy, happy, and growing.

To begin this journey, try the following exercise.

❖ Shut your eyes, get quiet, and conjure up a very positive image of yourself. Watch that Positive You get up in the morning, get dressed. If she has children, observe her getting them off to school. What are her interactions with her family like? What does she do for the rest of the day? Does she go to the same job you have (being a homemaker *is* counted as a job)? What are her interactions with other people? What kinds of things does she do over the course of the day? At the end of the day, what does she do? If she has a family, what are their interactions like? If she is single, whom does she see at the end of the day and how does she spend her evening?

Now turn your attention back to the Real You and tune in to how your body feels. Is there a sense of happiness or excitement at the prospect of the Positive You? Or frustration and defeat? Concentrate on what's going through your mind. You are likely to discover some thoughts, such as "My husband would never be as warm and loving as the Positive Me's husband." "My kids are so out of control, I'll never have the kind of smooth morning transition to school I imagine." "I hate my job and I'll never have the kind of interesting job that Positive Me has." "I just go home and feel sorry for myself and eat in the evenings, not like the Positive Me."

Focusing on the differences between the ideal or Positive You and the Real You can trigger ruminative overthinking, anxiety and despair, and escapist behaviors like bingeing, so you might be wondering, why should I do this exercise?[2] Because, before you can begin to make positive changes in your life, you have to be aware of the goals and expectations you hold for yourself, so that you can decide whether you really wish to hold them, or whether they are the legacy of society's expectations.

Some of the characteristics of the Positive You are likely to represent impossible goals that you have internalized based on society's messages about what you—and other women—should be. Was the Positive You skinny? Did she have a perfect relationship with her spouse, children, and coworkers? If so, you are likely to have discovered unreasonable expectations you have for yourself, either consciously or unconsciously. Striving to meet these expectations is not the solution—it's part of the problem that makes you depressed and want to escape through bingeing.

To illustrate the destructiveness of having impossible goals, or goals that have been set for you by other people, I want to tell you the story of Trin, a beautiful young Vietnamese-American woman I met when I was a professor at Stanford University.[3]

Trin arrived on move-in day at the dorm and announced amid the chaos that she was going to become a neurologist. It had been her dream since serving as a research assistant to a neurosurgeon in her hometown. The determination in Trin's eyes when she spoke of her goal made most of us back away from arguing that she should keep an open mind about her long-term future, especially given that it was her first day of college.

Trin drew much of her great strength of spirit from her family. The family had settled in the upper Midwest after escaping from Vietnam in the 1970s as members of the fabled "boat people." As Vietnam fell to the Communists, the family, including baby Trin and her six older brothers, packed into small boats and headed out to sea. All their material goods had been hastily sold, and the money converted into gold, which was sewn into the linings of her parents' clothes. Far away from shore, the boat sank in heavy seas. Trin's parents were forced to shed their coats, and thus their gold, to avoid sinking and drowning. Miraculously, a fishing trawler was nearby and saved the family. Several months and several refugee camps later, Trin and her family arrived in the United States and were "adopted" by a church in the Midwest. There they slowly rebuilt their lives, the father finding

work as a janitor, then a retail clerk, and finally a store man-
ager. From her preschool years, Trin's intelligence shone, but
she had to fight for her father's attention and respect, as the
youngest child and only daughter.

Then Trin was admitted to Stanford. This, coupled with
her experience of working with a neurosurgeon, crystallized
a dream she had of becoming a famous neurologist, wealthy,
internationally respected for her work, perhaps eventually a
professor at a major university. Trin didn't see any connec-
tion between this goal and her lifelong pursuit for her fa-
ther's love. Instead, it was a rational choice of careers, based
on her abilities and interests.

Trin certainly had the ability. She sailed through the biol-
ogy, chemistry, and physics courses required of premeds in
the first few years. But those of us who knew her well always
wondered if she had the desire. Although she could ace any
class she took, Trin never seemed to have the intrinsic passion
for her work that you like to see in anyone devoted to such an
ambitious goal. The only time her eyes lit up was when she
attended a poetry reading, occasionally held in the dorms, or
a visiting faculty member's lecture on the history of pioneer
women in the American Southwest. If, by some chance, Trin
didn't get the highest grade on an exam, she would come
back to the dorm and brood about it: "How could I have
been so stupid? Why didn't I study the chapter on quantum
mechanics more? I let myself get distracted—I'm going to
have to move out of the dorms so I can be alone and quiet to
get my studying done. But then I'll have to cook for myself

and that will take time away from my work. I've got to get moved to a quieter dorm, out on the edge of campus away from all the noise and activity."

Then in Trin's junior year of college, tragedy struck. Her father was killed in an automobile accident while driving home from work. Any loving child would be stunned and overwhelmed when they unexpectedly lose a parent. Trin, however, was not only overtaken by grief. She became a rudderless boat. She left school, not officially dropping out of class, just disappearing. She lost all sense of motivation to continue her studies or much of anything else in her life. She just hung out at her boyfriend's apartment, occasionally taking walks or watching a little television, much of the time staring out the window.

It was six months after her father's death when I next saw Trin. She was even thinner than before, and she had cut her hair short. Her eyes, though, were what I noticed. Gone was that look of steely determination, that "don't get in my way, I'm going to class" attitude. Instead there was a softness, a deepness, that I had only seen on those rare occasions when Trin was sitting quietly listening to classical music or reading a book of poetry instead of her biology textbook. I asked her what happened.

"I just floated for a couple of months. Thankfully, Sean [her boyfriend] kept me from self-destructing. I even thought of committing suicide a few times. I kept seeing my father, hearing him, when he wasn't there. He was trying to

tell me something, but I couldn't understand, I was so scared. I thought I was losing my mind." At this point, tears began running down her cheeks. "Then, several weeks ago, when I was asleep, I heard my father calling me: 'Trin, Trin, here, listen to me, daughter. Follow your heart. Follow your heart.' I couldn't tell if it was a dream, or what, I just knew I heard him, and I knew he said, 'Follow your heart.' But what did that mean? I lay awake the rest of the night, listening for his voice, asking him what he meant. But I heard nothing more, except the echo of his words, 'Follow your heart.'

"I spent a lot of time walking in the hills, still listening for my father. I was no longer seeing him or hearing him everywhere—it was as if he had spoken what he needed to tell me, and now he was really gone. I wanted him back, I wanted to ask him questions. But that was his way. He spoke something once, and only once, then he moved on. What was in my heart? I kept asking myself. No clear answers came except one—it wasn't medicine. Medicine wasn't in my heart. 'How could that be?' I asked myself. I've been driven toward medicine ever since high school. I'm very good at it. I could make a brilliant physician. But it was not in my heart. When I first realized this, I thought, 'I've lost my father, now I've also lost my calling, my career.'

"But instead of feeling empty and grieved, I felt a tremendous relief. It was as if something that had been holding me by the back of my neck for years had suddenly let go. My father had let go. He hadn't been the one holding on to

me exactly, it was what I thought he wanted of me, what I thought I had to do for him. And now he's gone. So my reason for pursuing medicine is gone."

I had always viewed Trin as a mature young woman, but I stood gaping in awe of her insight and growth. "What," I asked, "is going to replace medicine?"

"I don't know yet," she responded. "I'm coming back to school to find out. I've dropped the premed major and have declared an English major. My mother and brothers think I've lost my mind. But I think I've found it."

Trin eventually graduated from Stanford with a bachelor's and a master's degree in American literature, and went on to further graduate study. Her real accomplishment, though, was in letting go of a goal that was not truly hers but that was nevertheless running every aspect of her life— the goal of becoming a doctor. She could have achieved the goal. But because it wasn't in her heart, achieving it would not have given her rich and abiding pleasure.

Thankfully, most of us can readjust our expectations and goals for ourselves without having to experience a tragedy such as Trin's. First, ask yourself which of your goals you've picked up from society's messages or expectations other people have for you. Then ask yourself if those really reflect your values and the ways you want to define yourself. If the answer is no, then let go of them. Use your self-reflective strengths to imagine wrapping up these false gods in a bag, flipping the lid on the garbage can, and tossing them away.

Then rewind the tape of the Positive You's day. Shut your eyes, and before you play the tape again, say to yourself, "Be gentle. Be kind. Accept who you are. Be realistic." Then try running the tape again. How does the Positive You look different this time? Are there things about her that now look more like the Real You? Which characteristics of her or of her life bear little resemblance to the Real You? For example, perhaps the new Positive You still has quite a different relationship with her husband than you do. Or perhaps she has a pleasant evening without alcohol, when the Real You seems to need a drink to relax. Does she have energy and interest in what she does, while the Real You is always tired and unmotivated?

Rerun the tape a couple more times, and each time begin by telling yourself, "Be gentle. Be kind. Accept who you are. Be realistic." Notice which differences between Positive You and Real You keep coming back over and over, because those are likely to be the changes you want to make for yourself. Get a piece of paper and write each change down in the language of approach goals—new behaviors or ways of living that you want to move toward, rather than things you want to avoid or give up. Some examples might be "I want to eat three healthy meals a day." "I want to drink within healthy guidelines for women." "I want to increase my energy level." "I want to find a more interesting job."

Now you're ready to begin working toward these positive goals. In the rest of this chapter, I am going to give you some tools that will move you away from the toxic triangle and toward healthier living. These tools build upon those you learned to use in chapter 6 to identify triggers for depression, yo-yo eating, and heavy drinking. These new tools take you beyond what you learned in chapter 6 into a place where you are not just aware of your unhealthy habits and their sources but actively choosing new ways of thinking and behaving. These tools have been tested in research with women who suffer depression, eating problems, and drinking problems (or all three parts of the toxic triangle) and have been repeatedly shown to reduce their symptoms and help them make positive changes in their lives. The tools can also help you, no matter which combination of symptoms you suffer. If you believe you are on your way into the toxic triangle but haven't quite gotten there, these tools can help you turn toward a healthier place before you become trapped.[4]

Set the Stage:
Make Your Environment Healthier

It's difficult to move toward positive change if your environment keeps pulling you back into the toxic triangle. Let's focus first on simple changes you can make to reduce your likelihood of binge eating or drinking.

CLEAN YOUR HOUSE

Instead of dusting the furniture and mopping the floors, clean out those items that you believe are triggers or cues for overeating or drinking. Several of these triggers might have been identified while practicing mindfulness or in your diary. Maybe your binges often start with salty chips, or with a particular brand of cookies. Purge them from your pantry! You don't want to be tempted to binge on a luscious cake or pie, so you may want to skip cooking rich and fattening desserts until you've gotten control over your eating.

Replace your binge food with healthy snacks. Make sure you have plenty of fresh fruits and vegetables in the house. When you're shopping for food, make a list and stick to it. Don't go shopping when you're hungry or you'll be more likely to buy binge foods and to consume them. Instead of buying foods that can be taken out of their wrappers and eaten quickly, go for foods that take some preparation. You might try new recipes from books or magazines like *Cooking Light* that are focused on healthy eating.

You may also need to clean out your liquor cabinet or wine cellar, particularly if you tend to drink alone at home. If you don't want to dump out expensive liquor, give it to a friend. If your spouse or partner objects to your getting rid of the liquor, you may be able to move it to a place where it is less "in your face."

If your tendency is not to drink at home but at bars or parties, then for the time being you may need to limit your exposure to these tempting situations. This doesn't mean you can never go to a party again. But until you've gone for a while without over-drinking and have become accustomed to how your body feels after a pleasant evening without alcohol, it is best to keep your environment relatively free of it.

Eat a Square Three

You've heard it since you were a kid—eat three regular meals a day. Well, it's true. Eating three regular, normal-size meals a day is one of the best ways to avoid binge eating. (And binge drinking: many women drink when actually they are hungry—and become drunk much faster on an empty stomach.)

Don't wait until you are hungry to eat. If you've been dieting excessively or binge eating for a long time, your body's signals as to when it is empty or full are likely to be mixed up. Once you've been eating a reasonable amount on a regular schedule, you'll be able to trust these signals once again. But for now, set yourself a regular schedule of eating three full meals, say at 8 A.M., noon, and 6 P.M., and also schedule a light snack in between each meal.

"But I'll gain weight!" you might protest. This is unlikely. If you have a habit of starving yourself for long periods of the day, you are setting yourself up for binge eating. Even if you vomit or otherwise purge the binge, you still absorb significant calories from the food you have ingested. Eating three reasonable meals a day reduces the physiological and psychological drives to binge, making you likely to consume fewer calories per day than if you continue the habit of starving and bingeing.

If at all possible, plan your meals and don't let other things interfere with your eating times. At first, it doesn't matter so much what you eat as when you eat it. Establishing a regular pattern of eating can be very difficult for women who've gotten in the habit of grabbing a burger with their kids on the way to a game or skipping meals all day in an effort to control their weight. Use your family's health as a motivator if you need to—your kids need three square meals a day as much as or more than you do, and they will be more likely to eat healthfully if you do.

Try to concentrate on what you are eating during your meals and try not to do other things while you're eating. Mindless eating often leads to overeating. Use mindfulness techniques to notice everything about every bite—the texture, the heat or cold, the taste, how it feels as it goes into your mouth and down your throat. Research shows that people are much more likely to overeat if their minds are preoccupied with other tasks while they are eating.

Small Steps: Build New Activities

What do you do with all that time that you used to spend binge eating, drinking, or sitting around feeling depressed? It is critical that you build a new set of activities into your life that are healthy replacements for your former unhealthy behaviors. These can be simple, pleasant distractions that lift your mood and give you an alternative to bingeing. Or they can be endeavors that move you forward toward the changes you have decided you want to make in your life.

When you conjured up the realistic version of Positive You, what kinds of simple things did she do instead of drinking or eating? Perhaps she had a hobby or a sport. Perhaps she volunteered at a local charity. Perhaps you saw her lounging on the living room floor with her children, playing.

Make a list of simple, everyday things that you find enjoyable and that are relatively easy to do. These might range from taking a walk in your neighborhood to joining a recreational sports team. One of the most important steps to moving away from bingeing and toward a more Positive You is to find things to do that can take your mind away from your urges, filling up the time during which you would normally binge. Plan activities for the times between meals and snacks when you otherwise don't have anything to do. When you feel an urge to binge on food or alcohol, go back to something you've done and enjoyed before.

Finding pleasant endeavors to fill our time is also an important coping strategy for depression. In our research, we have found that just a few minutes of a pleasant, distracting activity can break up ruminative overthinking and lift a mood.[5] Breaking the grip of overthinking through pleasant distractions also improves the quality of your thinking, making it more positive and balanced and less negative and biased. Free of overthinking, you become a better problem solver, able to generate higher-quality solutions to your problems, and you have more energy to carry out these solutions. So although pleasant distractions may provide only short-term relief from overthinking and negative moods, they set the stage for longer-term relief by improving your abilities to overcome the myriad problems fed by overthinking.

In our studies, one of the most effective activities is exercise. Exercise provides a biochemical boost to your brain and a healthy distraction from overthinking and bingeing. Make sure to choose an exercise that is right for your body (you should talk with your doctor before starting anything new). Sports that require all your attention—like a challenging squash match or a technically difficult mountain climb—will do a better job of distracting you than those that can be done automatically and with little concentration.

Hobbies, such as glassblowing, gardening, model construction, or painting can be great distractions. Losing yourself in the activity is the key. Try something fresh that requires you to build new skills. Both hobbies and exercise can give you a sense of accomplishment and identity that shores you up and prevents you from falling back into the toxic triangle.

Bigger Steps: New Skills at Problem Solving

The activities you have come up with so far are meant to lift your mood, take you away from negative overthinking, and fill the time you would otherwise have spent bingeing. These are small steps, although critical ones, on the road to the Positive You. Now you are ready to take bigger steps—steps that will begin to overcome the larger problems in your life that drive your unhealthy thoughts and behaviors, and that help you reshape the Real You into the Positive You.

When you did the Positive You exercise, you developed a list of goals for positive change. These goals reflect your core values, what you want to be most true in your life. The toxic triangle takes you away from your core values. Bingeing, recovering from binges, or being depressed simply takes a lot of time that you could use to do things that are in line with your values. The social and psychological pressures that lead us into the toxic triangle, such as the demand that women be thin and that they sacrifice their needs for others, are goals that are imposed on you and often interfere with your pursuit of your own deeply held values. Here is an exercise to begin moving you toward those values.

❖ Take your list of approach goals—new behaviors or ways of living you want to move toward—developed in the Positive You exercise. Under each goal, brainstorm some things you can begin to engage in, today, that will move you toward your goals. Start small! Thinking you have to overhaul your behavior or your identity in one fell swoop will only set you up for defeat! What you write down first should be simple things that you can begin today, with the resources readily available.

Say, for example, that one of your goals is to do work that is more interesting and fulfilling than what you are currently doing. Some things you might consider doing to move toward this goal include:

1. Talk to friends who seem to like their work, to find out what it is that makes their jobs enjoyable.
2. Look through the "Help Wanted" ads in the newspaper or in a trade magazine for your profession to see what looks interesting.
3. Look into workshops or lectures on changing careers that might be given in your community, for example, at your local YWCA or community college.
4. Flip through the catalog for a local college to see what courses excite your interest, to get ideas of what direction you might want your career to go.

If you don't want to seek a new job but just want to spend your time in something more meaningful, you might think about volunteer work that is in line with your important values. Helping other people is a great mood lifter, as well as an important expression of what you believe. Volunteer to serve soup in a homeless shelter. Help an environmental group clean up a park. Take meals to an elderly person who can't leave her home. Your personal concerns will be cast in a different light after you've spent some time with the less fortunate.

Your larger problems or goals will require more advanced problem solving. Fortunately, psychological research has identified a set of problem-solving steps that can be applied toward a vast array of problems or goals, no matter how large.[6] Take one of your major goals, or a significant change you want to make in your life, and consider how you would apply each of the following steps:

1. List as many possible activities as you can to move you toward your goal without judging whether they are "good" or "bad." In other words, brainstorm things you can do without getting hung up on whether or not they'll work.
2. Now you get to judge how useful the behaviors you generated in Step 1 will be. Rank each one, considering how easy it will be to accomplish it and how effective it will be in moving you toward your goal. If you find yourself thinking, "That won't work! Nothing's

going to help!" try using the mindfulness techniques
learned in chapter 6 to slow yourself down and be
more open and gentle with yourself. Recognize that
the process of change is a gradual one and that there
are never any guarantees that changes we make will get
us to our goals. But you've made a commitment to
yourself to move toward the Positive You, and you deserve to live that way.

3. Once you decide what would be most helpful in
moving toward your goal, develop a plan to carry it
out. For example, if you've decided you need to take
some courses to improve your job skills and get a new
job, then the first step is to investigate a local educa-
tional institution. The second step is to sign up for a
relevant course. The third step is to take the course. It
may also be helpful to consider the available resources for each step. For example, you may need to
look into financial aid.

4. Schedule the first step in your plan. Scheduling simple
activities such as "Look up courses in the course catalog" may seem silly, but the act of scheduling will
make you more committed to carrying out the activity,
and will help ensure that you find the time to do it.

5. Once you go through with your scheduled activities,
evaluate how well they worked. How did they make
you feel? Did they accomplish what you wanted?

6. At this point, you may need to revise the plan, especially if you didn't get as far along the path to your
goal as you hoped. Again, be gentle and generous with
yourself—you won't get to the Positive You overnight,
just as you didn't travel into the toxic triangle
overnight. You may need to go back to Step 1 and repeat the process of generating ideas that move you toward your goal.

7. Whether or not everything you tried was successful, reward yourself for just trying. For example, treat yourself to a meal at your favorite restaurant or to coffee with a friend.

Build New Relationships

Women's empathy and strong emotional ties to others can lead them into the toxic triangle, but these strengths can also help them escape it.

ENLIST FAMILY AND FRIENDS IN YOUR GOALS

It's tough to make major changes in your life by yourself. Enlisting family members and friends as allies can significantly increase your chances of success. Simply making public your intention to change makes you more likely to stick with your plan when the going gets tough.

As discussed in chapter 6, loved ones can provide emotional support by listening and accepting your feelings of depression or anxiety, which can ease your own burden. They can be your cheerleaders as you make changes, encouraging you by their confidence that you will succeed. They can also be your safety valve—someone to call when you feel yourself sinking into despair, or giving in to the urge to binge.

Loved ones can provide practical support, in the form of sounding boards for ideas about the Positive You, and can help generate ideas about how to move toward the Positive You. They might also provide material support to help you accomplish your goals, for example, babysitting your children while you take a course to improve your job skills.

It's important that when you ask loved ones for help, you be specific, so they know what you need. You could say something like, "I've realized I have a tendency to binge eat [or drink too much at times] and I would like to be more healthy. Would you be willing to help me by . . ." and then finish the sentence with the kind of help that would be useful to you (such as being available for a phone call if you felt the urge to binge, rewarding you for going without bingeing for some specific amount of time, being tolerant with you if you become irritable as you first gain control over your binges).

Family and friends can also undermine your attempts to change. They may have a stake in you remaining the way you are. For example, if you've been shortchanging your own professional and intellectual needs in favor of your husband's career, he may view your new desire to pursue your own interests as a threat. Or, if much of your drinking happens in situations where your husband also drinks, he may feel that your attempts to cut back cast a negative light on his own behavior or that you are sending him a message to cut back on his own drinking.

People can also undermine your new goals by being insensitive. The friend who keeps pushing you to have one more glass of wine, or to eat more food when you're at her house, may be threatened by your willpower or may just be insensitive. A family member who expresses doubt that you'll ever finish your degree and pursue a new career may be threatened by the likelihood of your accomplishments.

In either case, it may be time to find new friends or to limit your time with unhelpful family members who make you feel more depressed than encouraged. People who are trying to abstain from alcohol often find that they cannot hang around with the friends they used to drink with and successfully resist the temptation to go back to their old behaviors. In part, this is because these friends often pressure them to drink. But what is not as well-known is that the body develops a physiological response to the environments in which you used alcohol that can make you crave a drink. This is called a *conditioned craving*. Because the characteristics of that environment—the look and smell of the bar, or specific people—are so often paired with the physiological effects of using alcohol, your body begins to go through physiological changes when you are in the environment, even if you are sober. The result of this environmental association is that your cravings can increase to a point where they can be difficult to resist. It may be necessary to avoid these environments and these people altogether if you want to abstain. It is easier to do if you've developed a set of alternate activities that are pleasant and in line with your values that can fill the time you used to spend in these triggering environments.

When the person who is undermining you is your spouse or someone you can't or don't want to avoid completely, it's time for you to become assertive. If your immediate response to this suggestion is, "Oh I can't. I can never stand up to him," or "He'll get mad and I can't stand that," then please realize that this excessive concern with relationships is what we identified in chapter 3 as a key factor pushing women into the toxic triangle. You are refusing to stand up to a friend or family member who is blocking your path out of the triangle and toward the Positive You for the sake of avoiding conflict.

Being assertive doesn't mean creating conflict, nor does it necessarily entail yelling at or blaming another person. What it does mean is making other people aware of the negative impact their behavior has on you, and asking them to change that behavior in a specific way.

❖ The major components of an assertive response are:

1. When you . . . (fill in the behavior that is undermining you),
2. it makes me feel . . . (fill in your specific feelings when this behavior happens).
3. I would like you to . . . (fill in a new specific behavior to replace the undermining behavior).

Let's go back to Peggy, whom we met in chapter 6, to illustrate an assertive response.

Peggy's husband, Lyle, offered her a drink when he got home from work even though she had told him she wanted to cut back. Peggy told Lyle, "No thanks. Like I said, I'm trying to cut down."

But he persisted. "Come on, Peggy, one little drink isn't going to hurt you. In fact, it will make you more relaxed. You seem really uptight and grumpy tonight."

Peggy felt her anger rising to the surface. How dare he try to bully her into drinking, insinuating that she needed a drink to be pleasant! How dare he push her to drink when she had explicitly told him she wanted to cut down!

"Lyle," Peggy said, as calmly and evenly as possible, "I feel really frustrated when you try to get me to have a drink with you when I've told you I'd like to cut down. It's very important to me that you support me in this. I'd like you to accept my 'no' as final when I say to you that I don't want a drink."

Notice that Peggy didn't expressly say that Lyle was being a jerk, though he was. If she had said this directly, Lyle would probably have become defensive or hostile. Instead, Peggy remained calm and voiced her concerns and feelings in as concrete a way as possible. She didn't ask him for some vague change in his behavior, such as "I want you to be more loving to me." Or "I want you to stop being such a jerk!" Asking for such nonspecific or huge changes in another person's character is asking for trouble. Instead, Peggy asked for a specific change that was well within Lyle's reach and would have a major impact on her ability to meet her goal of having evenings without alcohol.

Assertive responses not only stop the undermining behavior, they also make it easier for you to stick to the positive changes you are making in the way you eat and drink. The act of being assertive also has a major effect on your mood, making you feel more in control and less victimized. Some women find that becoming more assertive is an especially important component of overcoming the depression component of the toxic triangle. Self-assertion lifts them out of the sense of helplessness that is at the core of depression, while the act of becoming more assertive can have positive repercussions throughout a relationship, making those close to you more aware of, and sensitive to, your needs.

Assertive responses don't always work, however. Other people may not want to change, and may resist all your attempts to assert yourself and call for that change. They may even become hostile or angry. You can prepare for a negative reaction by anticipating the worst possible outcome of your own assertiveness, deciding ahead of time how you will cope with it. If you have any reason to expect that the other person will become violent toward you, then it's probably best not to proceed. Any relationship in which violence is a potent threat cannot be fixed by assertiveness; instead, please seek the help of a professional counselor to develop a plan to deal with this kind of relationship. You can find free help in most cities by calling programs for women in abusive relationships.

If the worst-case outcome of your assertiveness is that the other person becomes angry, refuses to even consider changing his or her behavior, and storms away, the first step in coping is to take care of yourself. In the past, you may have sunk into a deeply depressed mood or taken refuge in a drinking or eating binge. Now that you have decided to free yourself from the toxic triangle and pursue the Positive You, you need an alternative strategy. You might try reaching out to a friend for emotional support. You might want to use the mindfulness techniques or Diary Methods in chapter 6 to "be with" your feelings but not be overwhelmed or ruled by them, and to capture your thoughts as they flood your brain and body. The breathing exercises that are part of mindfulness can be very helpful in reducing feelings of frustration, anger, and anxiety.

The second step in coping is to decide how you will respond when others react to your assertiveness. In the past, you probably would have given in to any reluctance, believing nothing could change and it wasn't worth rocking the boat further. Don't do it! Giving in will only pull you back into the toxic triangle, eroding any progress you've made toward the Positive You.

It's best not to go running after your spouse, or whomever you have tried out your assertiveness with, to confront his or her disappointing response. The person may at this point be angry and not open to reason, at the same time that you've got a million angry thoughts flying through your head that are even less likely to help the situation. It is better to wait until you have formulated a calm, but again assertive, response.

So imagine that when Peggy made her assertive request to Lyle to change his behavior, Lyle reacted with hostility. Here's how she could assertively handle that situation:

Lyle initially was stunned at Peggy's response to his encouragement to have a drink. Then he got mad and shouted, "Ever since you got on this self-righteous kick of being on the wagon, you've been a real bitch!" Then he took his drink and stormed out of the room.

Peggy wanted to scream after him that he was an ass-hole and a drunk, but luckily she didn't. Instead, she continued to cook dinner, chopping vegetables furiously, and occasionally stopping to take some deep breaths and relax her body.

When dinner was ready, Peggy went into the family room, where Lyle was watching television. He didn't look up or acknowledge her when she walked into the room. She decided she didn't want this conflict to drag on through dinner, both of them sitting silently, trying to ignore each other. So she said, "Lyle, if I have been more irritable lately, I'm sorry. But even if I have, I don't think it is okay for you to press me to drink with you if I decide I don't want to. I don't want this to be an issue between us. But I don't want to feel like I have to drink just because you want me to."

Lyle replied, "I don't push you to drink. You drink because you like it. I just was being polite and asked you if you wanted a drink."

"You may not be intentionally pushing me to drink," Peggy said, "but when you keep encouraging me to drink when I've said I don't want to, it feels like you are pushing."

"Well, if that's how you feel about it," Lyle said reluctantly.

"Yes, that's how I feel about it," Peggy said firmly.

Lyle was a bit sullen through the first half of dinner, but by the time dinner was finished, he and Peggy were having a pleasant conversation about their plans for the upcoming holidays. The next evening, when Lyle came home from

work, he poured himself a drink but didn't encourage Peggy
to have one with him.

By formulating a response when you are calm, you will have the courage to assert yourself another time, rather than lose your nerve. It will also give you a set of coping tools, prepared in advance, that won't require you to react in the heat of the moment.

Use Your Powers of Empathy

As women, we break our backs to take care of others, and often can't understand why they don't respond with gratitude. But often people don't respond the way we would to a situation, or even the way they might want to. When we fall into a tailspin of over-thinking about how and why others behave as they do, it can lead us to become depressed, or to escape through bingeing.

We can instead use our empathy and emotional sensitivity to take a different perspective on the situation, as Jill did.

Jill was visiting her parents, and as usual her mother was pushing her to eat while her father was teasing her about how tight her pants were. What Jill would normally do, and what she felt like doing this time, was to go get another glass of wine and drown out her father's insensitivity, at the same time that she silenced her feelings of being fat, defective, lonely, and sad.

However, Jill had made a commitment to change. The yoga class she had been taking had helped her become aware of her body and her thoughts of self-loathing. She was tired of living in the toxic triangle and wanted to get more balance in her eating and drinking, and to stop letting her self-worth ebb and flow depending on what others said to her or what day of the week it was.

Jill considered blowing up at her dad, but instead she used her breathing exercises to slow down and give herself time to think about what might be a more effective response. She sat back and watched her dad. He could be such a jerk, and such a sweetheart. She couldn't understand how he could say such hurtful things to her and her sister. And then she realized she never would understand, nor could she ever change him, a seventy-five-year-old curmudgeon who had never been sensitive to others and never would be. What she could do was stop being around him. But she loved both her parents and didn't want to hurt her mother by breaking off ties altogether.

So she decided to do three things. One was to make some attempt to help her dad understand why she didn't want to hear him call her a "tub butt" again. The second was to limit her time with her parents—not to go over so often for dinner, even if doing so elicited her mother's protests. The third was to give up trying to change her father's personality to make him a more sensitive person. She could set limits on him, telling him there was to be "no more tub butt." And she would stop ruminating for hours on end about all the things he had said to her and how she wanted him to be different.

Jill was able to free herself from overthinking and the feelings of guilt and frustration inspired by her dad by accepting that she was not going to change his entire personality. In this way, Jill used her powers of empathy to shift her perspective on her dad and free herself from guilt and frustration, which in turn gave her the strength to draw the line with her father, assertively telling him that the "tub butt" refrain had to stop. This assertive response was Jill's way of taking care of and protecting herself. Jill was well on her way out of the toxic triangle.

Forgive and Move On

Another critical element of Jill's response to her father was to accept who he was, even to forgive him for it, and then move on. Forgiveness is not a popular idea in our culture. We're focused on justice and getting our due, and are encouraged by the media and people around us to take retribution on others rather than to forgive.

Yet at other times we want to understand why we have been unfairly treated. A huge amount of women's depressive ruminations is focused on questions like "How could he or she have done that?" We twist ourselves into knots analyzing the hearts and souls of those who have wronged us, trying to understand what caused them to behave as they did. Only sometimes do our powers of empathy give us the answers we need.

Most of the time we will never know the hearts and souls of others; even if we do, we may never accept their behavior. We *can* forgive them for it, however, which releases us from trying

to accept or understand it. Forgiving another person for their actions does not mean you condone those actions or deem that person to be acceptable. It also doesn't mean that the wrongdoer
should not be held accountable—you may still want to press
charges, file a lawsuit, or simply confront the wrongdoer. But forgiving means letting go of the desire for revenge for its own sake,
pulling away from the hold that anger and hatred have on your
heart and mind.[7]

The symptoms of depression, particularly guilt and shame,
sometimes signal that we need to forgive *ourselves*. Modern society
gives us endless reasons to feel contrite and embarrassed about
the things we have done to others and the choices we have made.
Understanding why you behave the way you do, of course, can
help you to avoid behaving in the same way in the future. But understanding yourself doesn't always bring relief from depression,
just as understanding why other people mistreated you doesn't always bring relief from anger. You may understand why you lied to
your boss when she asked if you completed your work, but still
feel guilty for doing so. You may understand why you blew up at a
friend who was just trying to be honest with you, but still feel
guilty the next time you see her. Here's where forgiveness comes
in. If we can forgive ourselves, we can move on to action, rather
than remaining mired in brooding and depression. When we forgive, we let go of our desire for revenge and retribution and focus
on recovery and repair, which is the first step down the pathway
toward health and well-being. Only then we will have the energy
and creativity to think of ways to move toward our positive selves,

and will be less likely to allow our guilty feelings to be transformed into anger against those who make us feel guilty.

You can use your powers of self-reflection and your mindfulness techniques to begin to forgive in this version of the Leaves Flowing Down a Stream exercise from chapter 6.

❖ Get quiet and comfortable and spend a couple of minutes focusing on your breath as it goes in and out. Imagine a stream running slowly by, and you standing on its banks. Every so often a leaf falls into the stream and begins to float with the current. Watch a few leaves float by and disappear down the stream. Now, as a leaf comes, place one of your thoughts concerning the person you want to forgive on that leaf. The thought might be specifically about something this person did. Or the leaf might hold your feelings about what was done. Or it might be a question about how could he have done that. Just start with whatever thought is easiest to place on the leaf. Then watch it float down the stream, getting smaller and smaller, eventually disappearing in the distance. When you are ready, place another one of your thoughts on a leaf and watch it go down the stream.

Keep doing this for as long as you wish—you may not be able to let all of your thoughts go in one sitting. They will come back. Just as the wind blows leaves around, your unforgiving, pained thoughts will return to you at times. If you still want to forgive and move on, go back to this exercise or another mindfulness exercise you find helpful, and once again let the thoughts go.

What makes an exercise like this work is not so much the mystical powers of mindfulness—it's the choice you've made to let go of hurt and to forgive. You may find other ways of doing this, perhaps through prayer or talking with a trusted friend or counselor. Or you may need to assertively confront the person who hurt you. Only you can decide what is best for you. But forgiving and moving on can be an essential step toward freeing yourself from the ghosts that keep pulling you into the toxic triangle.

Preparing for Lapses

I hope you've found some of the ideas for moving out of the toxic triangle and toward a more Positive You helpful. You're beginning to realize your expectations for yourself and which of these expectations you've chosen and which have been forced upon you by others. You're making choices as to which expectations you want to keep, and which you want to let go of. Armed with an image of your new, healthier goals, you've begun to practice activities that can move you toward them and work on close relationships that need to change. And you've taken some actions to initiate these changes.

What if, a day from now, a week from now, a month from now, you find yourself reverting to the unhealthy expectations, feelings, and behaviors that the toxic triangle generates? You may start to drink more, or more often, or may find it hard to resist the urge to binge eat. You are feeling out of control, or sad, or helpless.

It's tempting to react by saying to yourself, "I knew it wouldn't work! I knew I couldn't change!" This would only give you an excuse to go back to the same unhealthy ways that you previously used to cope with your feelings and thoughts. You may then give in and start binge eating or binge drinking, or sink into depression because "this is just the way I am."

You can prepare for these kinds of lapses, which are, after all, highly likely to happen. Preparing for lapses can take away some of their power and can impart weapons to fight the lapses should they occur.

The first step in preparing for a lapse is to take a card or a piece of paper and write: "A lapse is not a relapse. It is a momentary diversion. I can get back on the path to my Positive Me." You may want to use slightly different language, but the idea is to give yourself a concrete reminder that lapsing into your old behaviors for a short time does not mean that change is impossible, or that you have "relapsed" into the full-blown toxic triangle. You can make the lapse short term by cutting it off as soon as you notice it.

The second step in preparing for a lapse is to write down the techniques you have learned in this book or elsewhere that help you move away from toxic triangle behaviors and toward your new, healthier goals. Get a piece of paper, and list those techniques that worked for you in the form of commitments to yourself: "If I feel myself lapsing, I will . . . [use the Leaves Flowing Down a Stream exercise to gather my thoughts, begin to keep a diary of the thoughts I'm having when I'm being unhealthy, go talk to a trusted friend or counselor]." Be concrete—list specific techniques, perhaps even the page number where those techniques are described. In the future, if you feel yourself lapsing, you can pull out this list and use it to get yourself back on a healthier path. Lapse-prevention strategies have been shown in a great deal of research on people with depression, eating disorders, and alcohol addiction to significantly reduce the likelihood of severe lapses.[8]

Finally, and most important, realize that change is a process, not an end point. You are always changing, every day of your life, sometimes for the better, sometimes for the worse. If you cultivate the kind of compassion and respect for yourself that we've been talking about in these chapters, then you'll be able to weather setbacks.

Jill's story has a happy ending, because she was able to marshall her skills at self-reflection and empathy to understand some of the forces pushing her into the toxic triangle; then she transformed these skills into instruments for change. As she practiced meditation and made a commitment to change, she realized that her excessive drinking, yo-yo eating, and negative self-image were rooted in experiences with her family and in the unreasonable expectations she had for herself. Jill practiced assertiveness with her father, telling him how she felt when he teased her about her shape and weight. He protested, saying he meant no harm and that she was being overly sensitive. She stuck to her guns, though, asking him to refrain from his "tub butt" comments. Although he pouted for a few days, he did change his behavior, and their interactions improved. Jill also slowly built a new network of friends who weren't big partyers, but who liked to go to art galleries or hiking in the mountains, and who nurtured the healthier lifestyle she wanted for herself. Jill had setbacks: one particularly stressful week at work, she found herself reverting to heavy drinking to cope with thoughts that she was incompetent and hopeless. She recognized that she was careening down the path back into the toxic triangle, however, and called one of her new friends to talk about her fears and frustrations, and to get encouragement to get back on the path to her Positive Self. It wasn't easy and it wasn't quick, but Jill pulled herself out of the toxic triangle.

EIGHT

―――▼―――

Channeling Our
Daughters' Strengths

GIRLS OFTEN BEGIN to travel the path into the toxic triangle in adolescence. By the time they reach fifteen or sixteen,
many girls have suffered from substantial symptoms of depression, eating disorders, or alcohol abuse. By this age, girls have also
been well steeped in the societal pressures that push them toward
self-focused coping, excessive concern about relationships, and
dangerous expectations for themselves.

How can we help our daughters, our nieces, our young friends,
avoid getting trapped in the toxic triangle? Just as we can capitalize
on our own strengths of self-reflection and emotional sensitivity to
make changes toward more healthy coping and the fulfillment of
positive goals, we can help young women channel these same
strengths in themselves so that they make it through adolescence
and adulthood without fully reaching the toxic triangle.

Preaching at young women about what they shouldn't be, or how they shouldn't act, doesn't really help. Telling adolescent girls "Don't worry about your weight" or "Don't be concerned with what other people think about you" is like telling them not to breathe. Similarly, programs that merely "educate" young women about the dangers of alcohol, the social pressures for girls to be thin, or the symptoms of depression, don't consistently show positive effects.[1]

Instead we must encourage young women to develop their own goals—their own vision of a Positive Self—and the tools needed to move toward that vision.

Our Self-Reflective Powers Start Young

Picture an adolescent girl—maybe it's your daughter or another girl you know, or maybe it's an image of yourself as an adolescent—and watch her as she moves through a typical day. What does she spend a good deal of her time doing? If she's like many other adolescent girls, her day is likely to include:

1. Talking with her friends
2. Noticing what other people are doing
3. Thinking about herself and wondering what other people are thinking about her

Women's abilities to self-reflect and tune in to other people are formed at a very young age, and these tendencies are greatly amplified in adolescence. As a natural consequence of brain development, adolescents' minds become more capable of "thinking about thinking." As a result, they become obsessed with questions about how their own minds work, and why other people think and behave the way they do.

At the same time, adolescents become more oriented toward their peers, concerned about being accepted by them. Again, this is a natural consequence of biological development. Over evolutionary history, humans have usually begun to mate and raise families soon after puberty, which required becoming oriented toward the peer group from which they would select a mate.

An increase in self-consciousness and peer orientation occurs for both girls and boys in adolescence. But for girls, these increases are layered upon a predisposition toward self-reflectiveness and an orientation toward others and are present from early childhood. In addition, as we discussed in chapter 4, psychologist Jill Cyranowski suggests that increases in the hormone oxytocin during puberty lead girls to be particularly oriented toward relationships with others, to become more caring toward others, and to desire to be with and liked by others, especially their peers.[2]

As a result, adolescent girls are exquisitely attuned to the social scene around them. They can tell you who is doing what with whom and how all of their peers fit, or don't fit, into the social hierarchy. Every little nuance of social interaction catches their attention and is subject to analysis—a glance by a boy they are attracted to, the sneer of a girl who is more popular than they are, the mood of a close friend.

They are also exquisitely attuned to everything they do or say or think. They watch themselves behave as they move through the day, then hyperanalyze everything that happened, wondering what other people thought of them, or wondering why they act the way they do.

Moving from Reactivity
to Healthy Self-Awareness

Although tremendous sensitivity to others can make girls more susceptible to influence and unreasonable demands, their self-reflective strengths can also help them be aware of the effects others have on them. First and foremost, we need to help young girls recognize and respect the twinge or stab of discomfort they have in response to others. They need to take that discomfort seriously and listen to it, because it usually reflects the deeper values and goals they hold for themselves.

Too often, when a girl is uncomfortable with how others are behaving toward her, or what she perceives they want from her, she squelches this discomfort and focuses on changing her own behaviors to please them. This happens when girls suppress the anger invoked in them by others and get angry with themselves instead. It happens when they drink in an attempt to impress peers. It happens when they starve themselves trying to fit into some impossible image of what they are supposed to look like. After a while, a girl loses touch with what she thinks and feels, and becomes totally focused on "following the program" that she expects will make her successful with her peers. This is the trap that Patti, a short, blond, blue-eyed sixteen-year-old, fell into.

Patti was always trying to figure out what she was supposed to be doing. Her high school was a confusing and over-whelming place most of the time. It wasn't the academic work. She did well in most of her classes. It was the other kids. Patti felt as though they all understood how things were supposed to be—how to dress, how to act, whom to talk to, what extracurricular activities to get involved in. She wanted a guidebook on how to be a teenager.

Patti endlessly read magazines for teenage girls, trying to understand "the rules." Sometimes these magazines gave her hope. She would read articles with titles like "Ten Things You Can Do Now to Be More Attractive," and try to imple-ment these steps. Before long, however, she felt like a failure because either she couldn't carry out some of the steps or they weren't having the effect she wished.

On a recent weekend, Patti and her best friend, Carol, went to a party hosted by one of the popular kids, whose parents were out of town for the weekend. They normally wouldn't have been invited, but it was an "open house" party, so they decided just to walk in as if they were expected, although they avoided being seen by the host. Lots of the other kids were drinking heavily and some were smoking. Some guy Patti didn't know eased up next to her, and asked her if she wanted a drink. Patti hadn't drunk much before in the past, but she definitely didn't want to put this guy off, so

she said, "Sure." Patti felt nervous and unsure whether she
was doing the right thing, but Carol nudged her and encour-
aged her to go with the boy over to the bar.

Patti was so focused on doing what was "right" by standards set by others that she couldn't recognize and respect the signs within herself that what she was doing might not be right by her own standards. Girls become very good at shutting out awareness of what they are really feeling, and instead pay close attention to what others want them to feel.

We can help girls use their strengths at self-reflection to tune in to and respect their own feelings and thoughts. We can do this by helping girls become more mindful. Show your daughter chapter 6 of this book, and suggest she give the mindfulness exercises in it a try. You could sign up for a course on meditation or yoga with her.

Pushing a girl to become more mindful and meditative when she doesn't want to, however, won't work. Mindfulness must be entered willingly, particularly if your daughter is already showing signs of entering the toxic triangle, she may resist all forms of direct intervention.

We can indirectly cultivate mindfulness and self-respect in our daughters by being more mindful in our own interactions with them. We can use mindfulness techniques to listen to girls nonjudgmentally and with compassion. This, in turn, will help them listen to themselves more closely and compassionately, to recognize the thoughts and feelings that are driving their unhealthy behaviors, and feel freed to make alternative choices.

There are some fairly simple ways to become more mindful in listening to others.[3] First, it is important to be aware of your own emotional reactions to what your adolescent girl is saying. Nothing can create emotional arousal or distress faster in a parent than hearing her teenager talk about an upsetting situation. This is especially true if you perceive the situation to be dangerous or threatening.

Imagine, for example, that you are Patti's mother, and she comes home obviously having drunk alcohol, quite upset, and wanting to talk about it. It can be difficult to remain calm enough in this situation to identify your primary emotional responses. Accurately labeling your responses is key, however, for an appropriate and compassionate response to the situation.

If you were Patti's mother, you would likely feel anxious and worried about her. These are your primary emotions. While these emotions reflect your compassion and wish to help, you may also feel angry toward Patti. Anger is, then, a secondary emotion—one that is a learned, defensive reaction to your feelings of worry and fear. Anger is usually based on a judgment of another person. As soon as judgments enter an interaction, there is a likelihood that emotions and conflict will escalate.

Your goal in mindful listening is to let go of judgments so that you can hear what the other person is saying and feeling. One way to do this is to consciously remind yourself, as you feel your emotional arousal level go up, "This is my child, whom I love," or "I love her enough I want to work this out together." It's a good idea to practice saying these things to yourself when you are not upset or aroused. Then in the heat of the moment you'll be more likely to use this kind of self-talk to calm yourself down. You might also want some cues to remind yourself to engage in self-talk in difficult times. For example, you might wear a thin bracelet or necklace that your daughter gave you, which reminds you of her, so that when you begin to feel upset, you can touch this object to cue yourself to breathe, and engage in self-talk. If you don't want to wear something, you might practice engaging in slow breathing and self-talk each time you see your daughter make some gesture she always makes when she is upset, such as shaking her head or scrunching up her eyes.

Just because you want to listen compassionately and really hear what your daughter is telling you, doesn't mean you have to agree with what she says or does. You can remain very clear about your own standards for her behavior. Mindful listening, however, will help keep the lines of communication open, making it more likely that you will know what she's up to and how she's thinking, which in turn will foster her belief that you understand what's happening to her. Fortunately for Patti, her mother, Julie, used mindful listening to respond to her when she came home from the party tipsy, and then made it clear that the family's value system did not include a teenage daughter becoming drunk.

Patti tried to slink in the back door but, unaccustomed to handling alcohol, made a lot of noise. Her mother came down to investigate and found Patti sitting on the kitchen floor, leaning against the cabinets, a tear slowly rolling down her cheek. At first Julie was alarmed: "Honey, what happened, what's wrong?!"

Then Julie smelled the alcohol on Patti's breath. Her immediate reaction was anger, even rage. Julie's dad had been an alcoholic, and to smell alcohol on Patti felt like the fulfillment of her worst nightmare. Just before she was going to yell at Patti, though, Julie drew in a deep breath, shut her eyes, and said to herself, "She's not my father. She's my daughter. I want to keep my cool."

Patti started to tell Julie about her evening: "There was this guy. At a party." Patti started crying more vigorously at this point, and put her head in her hands. The thought that raced through Julie's mind was that Patti had been assaulted. She started to interrupt to demand the boy's name, but again she caught herself, took another deep breath, and said, "Okay, and what happened?"

"He came over to talk to me. And he offered me a drink. I didn't really want to, but he was really cute and I didn't want him to think I was dumb. So I had a drink. And then we kept talking, and I kept drinking. Mom, I just want to throw up! Please make my head stop spinning!"

Julie still needed to know the rest of the story. "Did anything else happen with this guy?"

"No, after a while he went over to talk to some other girl. Carol brought me home. Oh, Mom, it doesn't matter what I do, boys just aren't interested in me!"

Julie had a feeling that anything she said at this point wouldn't register with Patti, so she responded, "I know you're miserable right now, honey. Let's get you to bed and we'll talk about this tomorrow."

After Patti had slept off a nasty hangover, Julie sat her down to talk about why she thought she had to drink to impress this boy, as well as her more general feelings of being inadequate compared to the other girls. Near the end of the conversation Julie said calmly, but firmly, "Patti, drinking isn't a good solution for anything. Particularly in our family. Let's talk about what you could have done differently when that boy offered you a drink."

A good time to practice mindfulness with your loved ones is when you're *not* upset with them. You'll learn a great deal about your daughter if you stay quiet and listen. You'll also be more likely to listen to her mindfully during stressful times if you've had practice doing so during calmer times. This may involve slowing the pace of your life enough so that there is time to listen mindfully. Teenagers tend to be chronically on the go these days, as are parents, and often there is little time left for mindful listening. Even when parents and children are together, we are usually focused on ourselves to a large extent, rather than being intently focused on those we are with. So when you are talking with your adolescent before school, pour all your attention into what she is saying, the inflections in her voice, how she moves her head, and what messages her body is giving. Don't interrupt to give her advice. Don't bring up past arguments or transgressions. Just try to listen and nonjudgmentally acknowledge what she is saying.

Notice your own emotional reactions to your daughter, but don't act upon them. Just describe them with acceptance, either to yourself, or out loud. "It makes sense that I get anxious, then angry, when she talks about that boy I don't like." Acknowledging your own emotions will help you keep them in check so you don't say things that will shut down lines of communication. You may also notice happy emotions in yourself when you listen to her—a sense of pride when she tells you about an accomplishment, a recognition of her maturity in handling a situation. As parents we often spend all our energy noticing and trying to correct what is wrong with our children, rather than celebrating what is right. Appreciating our children's strengths, however, can keep us more balanced as we confront their weaknesses.

Mindful listening and the insights it gives you into what your daughter is thinking and feeling are just the beginning. The message you send that you care about her and want to understand her, and that her thoughts and feelings are valid, will help her accept herself and value her own needs and wants above the demands of others.

If your daughter is following the path into the toxic triangle, mindfulness will need to be accompanied by change—in her behaviors toward eating and drinking, in the activities she engages in, and in the expectations she has for herself. Fortunately, research has shown that we can prevent or reduce depression, eating disorders, and alcohol abuse in adolescents and young adults.[4] There are two general characteristics of effective intervention programs for these problems in this age group. The first helps young people learn and practice new skills to control their behaviors and cope in healthy ways with stress. The second challenges destructive attitudes that support the toxic triangle.

Learning New Skills

As I mentioned earlier, programs that attempt to steer adolescents and young adults away from excessive drinking or disordered eating behaviors, or try to prevent depression simply by preaching at them, tend not to work well. For example, many colleges have programs to reduce drinking and drinking-related problems among students, which emphasize the health-related consequences of drinking. Such long-term concerns do not impress young people, who are more likely to be focused on the short-term gains of drinking alcohol. Providing information about the dangers of alcohol abuse, trying to invoke a fear, likewise has little effect.

Similarly, programs that inform young women about what a healthy diet is and about the dangers of excessive dieting or bingeing are not effective.

Instead, programs that help young people to identify the triggers for their unhealthy behaviors, and learn skills to avoid giving in to these triggers, meet with more success. For example, if your daughter is bingeing frequently or dieting excessively, try some of the strategies discussed in chapters 6 and 7 to help her move toward healthier eating habits. Encourage her to keep a diary of her thoughts and behaviors around food. What are the situations that are most likely to trigger binge eating or, on the other hand, skipping a meal? Clean your house of binge foods. Get yourself and your family organized to have regular meals together. This will help normalize her eating schedule and give you opportunities to listen mindfully to her concerns and daily activities. Take stock of your own eating habits and attitudes toward food and weight. Are you setting the right example for healthy eating? Do you voice concerns about your own weight that reinforce your daughter's concerns about hers? Are there other members of your family who undermine your daughter's attempts to eat reasonably or who fuel her concerns about weight and shape? Be willing to be your daughter's "eating buddy" by starting a healthy eating plan with her and encouraging her attempts to take positive control over her eating habits.

SKILLS TO OVERCOME OVERTHINKING

If your daughter seems vulnerable to depression and overthinking, there are many tips in my book *Women Who Think Too Much* for learning new coping skills to interrupt the cycle of overthinking and reduce depressive symptoms. I'll summarize some of them here.

The first critical step is to break the grip of overthinking. When we overthink, it's as if all the nodes in our brain that hold negative thoughts are lit up and communicating with one another. Your daughter may begin a bout of ovethinking by rehashing something her friend said to her at school earlier in the day. Then her thoughts might move to the argument she had with her father at dinner. Then she might look at her homework and think, "I can't do this! It's too much! I'll never get better grades anyway!" This cascade of negativity brings with it overpowering feelings of helplessness and hopelessness, and with them the symptoms of depression. These feelings fuel negative thoughts and allow the overthinking cycle to strengthen and perpetuate.

This cycle can be broken, however, with remarkably simple activities. The key lies in doing something that will take her mind away from her negative thoughts, even for a short while. In my research, I have found that giving people positive distractions from brooding for just eight minutes is remarkably effective in lifting mood and breaking the cycle of repetitive thought.[5] We asked people who were in a depressed mood to do one of two tasks. The overthinking task focused their attention on their moods and thoughts. Specifically, we gave them 45 index cards, each printed with a phrase like "Think about your level of motivation right now" or "Think about how your life has been going lately." We asked each person to focus intently on the cards and what they said.

The other task was a distraction task that drew their attention away from their brooding to pleasant thoughts or images that had nothing to do with their emotions or with self-evaluation. These cards had phrases like "Think about a cloud formation in the sky" and "Think about a cool fan blowing on you on a warm day."

After eight minutes, the depressed people who had done the overthinking task were even more sad and depressed than they had been at the beginning of the experiment. Those who had done the distraction task, however, experienced substantial relief from their negative feelings—indeed, their moods became quite normal, according to their own ratings. This was despite the fact that the two groups—those who did the overthinking task and those who did the distraction task—were equally sad and depressed at the beginning of the experiment.

Even more important, we found that breaking the hold of overthinking by focusing on pleasant distractions improves the quality of people's thinking, making them more positive and balanced, and less negative and biased. It also improves their problem solving, making them better able to think of solutions to their problems and more energized to carry these solutions out. So though pleasant distractions may provide only short-term relief from overthinking and negative mood, they set the stage for long-term relief by improving people's ability to overcome the problems they ruminate over.

We all have our favorite distractions. For some people it's reading an engrossing book. For others, it's exercising or taking a brisk walk. For others, it's interacting with their children or friends who take their mind away from themselves. One friend of mine says that gardening is her lifesaver, because she can put all her energy and attention into it for long periods of time. In our research, we generally find that physical activity makes distraction more effective, probably because it's more difficult to continue to brood when you are active, and perhaps because physical activity has some positive biochemical effect on the brain.

For some women, and for some of our daughters, binge eating or drinking is a favorite distraction. Obviously, these are part of the toxic triangle, not an escape from it. Help your daughter find some new, positive activities to engage in when she's tempted to turn to food or drink to get her mind off her raging ruminations.

Work on developing these new activities when she's not in the depths of despair—heading for the refrigerator or sneaking a beer—so that they can be established as part of a toolbox of strategies for halting her advance toward the toxic triangle.

Another way to break the grip of overthinking is to "hand it over"—letting go of the negative thoughts through prayer or meditation. One woman I know literally cups her hands and holds them out as she prays to God to take her worries and concerns. The mindfulness exercise Leaves Floating Down a Stream can have a similar effect. Or you or your daughter might try dumping your concerns on paper or the computer. Writing worries down can release you from some of their power, and the act of putting concerns into words can make them more concrete and easier to manage.

One of the activities for letting go of ruminations that readers of *Women Who Think Too Much* especially liked was to schedule overthinking times. I know it sounds gimmicky, but it works extremely well. If you find yourself overthinking during the day, say at work, or notice that your daughter tends to overthink at school, put a stop to it by scheduling a time when overthinking can be resumed later in the day without interfering with work or school. The magical thing is that when it comes time for your overthinking hour, your concerns seem smaller and more manageable because you've broken the grip overthinking has on your mind.

The second critical step in overcoming overthinking is taking action to change the situations that lead you into overthinking and depression. To do this, you and your daughter may need to learn new skills at problem solving. I listed the steps of effective problem solving in chapter 7. Essentially, they can be summarized as:

1. Generate as many possible solutions to your problem or ways you can change a difficult situation, without prejudging any of them.
2. Rank order your list, from best to worst, in terms of the likelihood that the solution will have a positive effect; or rank them in terms of feasibility.
3. Make a plan for how to carry out your best solution, and schedule when you are going to act on each step of your plan.
4. Carry out each step, then evaluate how well each worked.
5. Reward yourself for carrying out the steps, regardless of whether they worked as you wanted them to.

Let's see how Julie, Patti's mother, whom we met earlier in this chapter, could use these steps in helping Patti deal with her problem of "the boys aren't interested in me."

Julie decided that one of the important ways to help Patti was to deal with her expectation that she needed to drink in order to be attractive to boys. So one day when they were talking together and both in relatively good moods, Julie asked Patti, "Honey, maybe we could think of some things you could do to get to know more boys. Do you have any ideas?"

Patti got a bit defensive and said sarcastically, "I could be like the popular girls. I could drink. I could wear sexy clothes. I could flirt. But you wouldn't let me, and I probably would screw it up anyway, just like at that party!"

Julie recognized that this conversation could turn hostile quickly, so she paused for a moment, tried to calm herself, and said, "No, that doesn't really sound like you. I wonder if there are other things you could do, things you would like to do, that would give you more chances to meet boys who like the same things?"

This came as a bit of a surprise to Patti—she had thought her mother would get annoyed at the sarcasm in her previous remark. She thought for a bit, then said, "Well, I like writing. I've wondered if I might be able to be on the school newspaper, or the yearbook. And I like singing. But I don't know how to join. They probably wouldn't take me anyway."

Staying patient, Julie said, "Well, what are some things you can do today to find out about the newspaper, or the yearbook, or the singing clubs at school?"

"I guess I could ask the teachers who are advisors for the clubs," Patti responded. "I could also ask some kids who are in the clubs." Julie agreed these were great ideas, and got out the school handbook to see who the faculty advisors for the clubs were. Patti was somewhat resistant, but Julie persisted and soon they had the names of several people Patti could talk to about different clubs.

A few months later, Patti was involved in the school cho-

rus and writing for the newspaper. She was meeting lots of new teenagers, boys and girls, who had interests similar to her own.

SKILLS AT CHANGING DANGEROUS DRINKING BEHAVIORS

If your daughter has succumbed to binge drinking, you may be especially panicked and unsure of what to do. What you may want to do is to prohibit her from drinking, but short of locking her in her room for the rest of her life, you're unlikely to be able to stop her altogether.

We can get some good ideas for how to help our daughters learn to control, and with hope eventually stop, dangerous drinking behavior from successful programs designed to curb drinking in college students. One such program is the Alcohol Skills Training Program (ASTP), developed by psychologist Alan Marlatt and colleagues at the University of Washington. This program views young drinkers as relatively inexperienced in regulating their use of alcohol and in need of skills to prevent abuse. In this program, learning to drink safely is likened to learning to drive safely; you must learn to anticipate hazards and avoid unnecessary accidents. This is referred to as a *harm reduction model* of intervention.

Based on the harm reduction model, ASTP targets heavy-drinking college students for intervention. Students are first taught to be aware of their drinking habits, including when, where, and with whom, by keeping daily records of their alcohol consumption and the situations in which they drink. They are also taught to calculate their own blood alcohol levels; it often comes as a surprise to people how few drinks it takes to be legally intoxicated.

Next, students' beliefs about the "magical" effects of drinking on social skills and sexual prowess are challenged. They discuss the negative effects of alcohol on social behaviors, on the ability to drive, on weight, and on hangovers. Students are encouraged to set personal goals for limiting alcohol consumption based on factors such as their maximum blood alcohol levels and desire to avoid the negative effects of alcohol. Abstinence is not insisted upon, but it is accepted as a good goal for many students. Skills for limiting consumption include alternating alcoholic and non-alcoholic beverages and selecting drinks based on quality rather than quantity, such as buying two good beers rather than a six-pack of generic beer. In later sessions, members are taught to consider alternative ways to reduce negative feelings. Instead of drinking alcohol, students are taught relaxation exercises to reduce sources of stress in their lives. Finally, in role-playing exercises, participants are taught skills for avoiding high-risk situations in which they are likely to drink too much, as well as skills for resisting peer pressure to drink.

Evaluations of ASTP have shown that students decrease their alcohol consumption and the problems that go along with it, and an increase is seen in their social skills resisting alcohol abuse.[6] In one study, Marlatt and colleagues intervened with high-risk drinkers at the time they might be most open to intervention, in their first year of college.[7] They identified a group of high school students who were about to enter the University of Washington who were already drinking at least monthly, consuming at least five to six drinks in one sitting, or who reported frequent alcohol-related problems. These high-risk students were then randomly assigned to receive either a one-session intervention based on the Alcohol Skills Training Program or no intervention, sometime in January through March of their first year of college. Both groups of students were followed for the next two years.

Over those two years, the intervention group showed less drinking overall and fewer harmful consequences of drinking (for example, getting into alcohol-related accidents) than did the comparison group. In addition, approximately 90 percent of those receiving the intervention said it was helpful and that they would recommend it to friends.

We can translate the methods of ASTP to help our daughters avoid the unhealthy use of alcohol. The first step is to acknowledge that they are, or may be, using alcohol. Denying that they are using, or just yelling at them to stop, will not be helpful to you or to them. The next step is to help them understand what circumstances lead them to use alcohol. Is it when they are upset? Is it because they are pressured by other kids? When they drink, what are they hoping the alcohol will do for them? Do they believe they can handle alcohol? Is there evidence that they can't (such as missing school because of hangovers)?

Based on the answers to these questions, you can help your daughter develop a realistic plan for avoiding the situations that lead her to drink, and particularly to binge. Since so many women, young and old, drink in response to social pressure, part of this plan should include practicing how to assertively refuse a drink when another person insists (refer back to the strategies for assertive responses in chapter 7). Another part of the plan may involve developing friendships with other young women who don't drink and engaging in activities centered around your daughter's values, such as a sport, hobby, or volunteer activity. These activities will serve as diversions from drinking and will help lift negative moods. They will also help move your daughter toward a positive image of herself and her values.

Challenging Destructive Attitudes

Another key ingredient in programs that have successfully prevented the toxic triangle in young people is challenging the destructive attitudes and self-expectations that undergird the triangle. These include the belief that you must be very thin to be attractive, that you must put others' needs before your own, that you must meet unreasonable conditions in order to feel good about yourself, and that you must always have complete control over yourself.

To challenge these harmful attitudes, we must recognize and acknowledge them in ourselves first. The mindfulness and diary strategies in chapter 6 can help you and your daughter identify what kinds of thoughts and expectations are driving damaging behaviors and moods. Then what do you do?

A standard technique in successful therapies for depression, alcohol problems, and eating disorders is to challenge a client's negative thoughts by asking her what the evidence is for and against these thoughts. For example, let's say your daughter tells you that girls who drink alcohol at parties are more popular. You might ask her for some examples, which she could no doubt name. Then you might ask her whether there are any girls who don't drink at parties who are popular. When she names a few girls, you can talk about why they are popular. You can also ask her whether there are girls who drink a lot at parties but who are not popular. You can explore with her the possibility that these girls are not popular in part because of their unappealing behavior when they are drunk.

Particularly with adolescents, you can find yourself arguing until you are blue in the face over whether there is good evidence for their attitudes or expectations. At that point, a more effective tactic is to help our daughters understand that they have a choice in how they are going to think about themselves, and the expectations they are going to hold for themselves. It may be true that boys are more attracted to girls who are thin, but is this something they want to hold themselves to? It may be true that they aren't getting the grades they want to have, but do they want to let this make them miserable for the rest of their lives?

Your daughter may protest that she can't just decide to think about herself and her life a particular way! Here's where you can protest right back, and give her solid evidence that it is possible to choose your attitudes and perspectives, even in the most dire of circumstances. A number of powerful books have been written by people who have had every reason to despair, but who actively chose a positive perspective on themselves and their situations. A classic example is Viktor Frankl's *Man's Search for Meaning*. Frankl was imprisoned in Nazi concentration camps during World War II, and faced starvation, torture, and the loss of his father, mother, brother, and wife. Even in the total misery of the concentration camp and the constant degradation of his humanity by Nazi guards, he was able to choose his perspective on himself and on his conditions. He wrote: "Everything can be taken from a man but . . . the last of the human freedoms—to choose one's attitude in any given set of circumstances, to choose one's own way."[8]

A more contemporary example is *Reading Lolita in Tehran*, by Azar Nafisi. Nafisi resigned from her job as a professor of literature at the University of Tehran in Iran in 1995, due to the repressive policies of the government against women. For two years, she invited seven young women to her home to read great works of literature by Vladimir Nabokov, F. Scott Fitzgerald, Jane Austen, and others. These books were officially banned, so the women met in secret. Many of the women were shy and intimidated at first, but over the course of two years they used the books they read as a backdrop for discussions of their lives and the political and social situations in Iran. They then began to strike out in their own ways against authoritarianism and repression. Writes Nafisi: "There, in that living room, we rediscovered that we were also living, breathing human beings; and no matter how repressive the state became, no matter how intimidated and frightened we were, like Lolita we tried to escape and to create our own little pockets of freedom."[9]

Books like this can help our daughters put into perspective the pressures they face in their own lives and can embolden them to reject the stifling attitudes they have absorbed from their peers and elders. If your daughter isn't much of a reader, you might read books like these yourself, and pull examples or quotes out of them to use in your conversations with her. Or you might arrange for your daughter to talk with someone you believe is especially good at defining herself or himself independent of others' expectations, such as an adult in your church, synagogue, or mosque.

Eradicating the Toxic Triangle

Just as we must work together to eradicate diseases such as HIV, we must work together to eradicate the toxic triangle. As with any disease, the process begins with our own attitudes and behaviors. With HIV, if we are not practicing safe sexual behaviors, then we can become infected with and transmit HIV. With the toxic triangle, if we've bought into the ideal of extreme thinness for women, or always expect ourselves or other women to cope quietly and privately with their problems, we then perpetuate the toxic triangle by allowing the conditions that support it to go unchecked. If we're trapped in cycles of depression, dieting and binge eating, and heavy drinking, we won't have the resources to respond to the toxic triangle in our daughters and women friends. Thus we owe it to our daughters, friends, and granddaughters, as well as to ourselves, to do what we need to do to overcome the toxic triangle in our own lives. I hope this book has given you some ideas. You may also wish to seek the help of others—friends, clergy, or mental health professionals—to fully break free of the triangle.

As you are personally freed from the toxic triangle, you will begin to see how the social and psychological causes of the triangle permeate our society. Spend a day noting how often you see advertisements or magazine articles that promote thinness in women. Jot down TV programs or movies that depict independent women as bitches, while caring, self-sacrificing women are depicted as "nice." Listen for "should" messages about how you, or your daughter, or women in general are expected to behave.

Confront these messages when they come from your friends and family members. Often they won't realize the attitudes they take for granted and then voice to other women, so making them aware can go a long way toward changing their behavior. Other times you may have to be more persistent and demanding of those around you. If they choose not to change, you may have to limit their impact on you or your daughter by limiting exposure to them.

Challenge society's unhealthy messages to women through what you buy and wear. Cancel your subscriptions to offending magazines and tell them why. Turn off TV shows or walk out of movies that glorify harmful images of women. If you have a choice, don't send your daughter to a school that makes it clear that they are less valued than boys.

Organize discussions in your community, your religious group, or your daughter's school about the toxic triangle and how to prevent it. Bring in local experts on women's mental health to talk about the toxic triangle. Lead discussion groups about the phenomenon of the toxic triangle so that others can confront it and talk about how to eliminate it.

Agitate in your community for activities that provide girls with positive alternatives to the toxic triangle. Examine your daughter's school to see if girls have equal access to sports, clubs, leadership posts, and other activities that can build their strengths. Find out about school cliques that promote unhealthy expectations for girls—such as excessive thinness or drinking like a guy—and work with the school to respond effectively.

Finally, realize that overcoming the toxic triangle, in yourself or in society, takes a great deal of persistence and dedication. Learning a few new self-help strategies, or organizing a few lectures in your community, won't defeat the pervasive conditions that perpetuate the triangle. Within ourselves, we need to constantly revise and strengthen our vision of the Positive Self we want to become, generating ideas for how to move toward her while understanding the obstacles we face in doing so. We will have lapses back into dangerous drinking, unhealthy eating, and debilitating depression. These lapses do not mean we have failed, or that conquering the toxic triangle is impossible. They simply mean we are human, and under tremendous pressure to think and behave in ways that, as women, jeopardize our health and well-being. But as women, we can turn our vulnerabilities into strengths, using our powers of self-reflection to recognize the forces driving us into the toxic triangle, while choosing to turn away from them toward health.

Resources

———————▼———————

There are many good sources of information available on mental health, eating disorders, and alcohol consumption. I offer a combination of straightforward self-help resources and more personal stories. A few that I recommend:

EATING

Overcoming Binge Eating by Christopher Fairburn
This is a step-by-step self-help guide to dealing with binge eating by one of the leading researchers in the field. Fairburn's prescriptions are based on sound research on what helps people overcome binge eating.

Binge No More: Your Guide to Overcoming Disordered Eating by Joyce Nash
This practical handbook is divided into five sections. Topics include defining binge eating, its potential harm, and its biological and societal causes; how to assess and alter binge patterns; how to change the thoughts that fuel those patterns; the role of medication; and advice on when to consider therapy or other professional help.

Overcoming Overeating by Jane R. Hirschmann and Carol H. Munter
An excellent, straightforward guide to overcoming the diet/binge cycle.

It's Not about Food: Change Your Mind; Change Your Life; End Your Obsession with Food and Weight by Carol Emery Normandi
Starting with the assumption that weight problems are as much emotional as physical, this book teaches techniques for becoming attuned to the body, setting personal limits, and understanding what is emotional—and not physical—hunger.

The National Eating Disorders Association (www.nationaleatingdisorders.org)
The organization can provide you with information on binge eating and other eating disorders, as well as referrals, support groups and hotlines, conferences and newsletters.

Mirror-Mirror (www.mirror-mirror.org)
This is a useful resource for individuals and loved ones on the way to recovery—providing a useful list of symptoms and relapse warning signs.

Memoirs and a Novel

Wasted: A Memoir of Anorexia and Bulimia by Marya Hornbacher
A haunting memoir from a young woman who suffered severe anorexia and bulimia.

Hunger Point by Jillian Medoff
This novel tells the story of two sisters battling eating disorders with humor and insight.

Stick Figure: A Diary of My Former Self by Lori Gottlieb
After finding the diary she kept when she was eleven years old, Gottlieb wrote this moving chronicle of her childhood struggle with anorexia.

DRINKING

Responsible Drinking: A Moderation Management Approach for Problem Drinkers by Fredrick Rotgers, Mark F. Kern, and Rudy Hoetzel
The tips in this book are based on a model of intervention for alcohol problems that has significant support. The book includes many case studies and exercises to help readers identify their triggers for drinking and develop alternative lifestyles.

Controlling Your Drinking: Tools to Make Moderation Work for You by William R. Miller
Clear, concise, non-judgmental, and practical, this book lays out techniques for moderation and self-discovery.

Moderation Management (www.moderation.org)
This is a behavioral change program and national support network providing a mutual help environment that encourages people who are concerned about their drinking to take action to cut back or quit drinking before the problems become severe.

Addiction Alternatives (www.addictionalternatives.com)
Espousing a philosophy of self-empowerment, based on therapist Marc Kern's research, this site provides further reading, free consultation, and information on support groups and resources around the country.

Alcoholics Anonymous (www.alcoholics-anonymous.org)
This well-known organization provides support and meetings around the world.

Memoirs

Drinking: A Love Story by Caroline Knapp
A wrenching account of Knapp's struggles with alcoholism, eating disorders, and depression. Her symptoms are much more severe than many readers', but the co-occurrence of alcohol problems, eating disorders, and depression in this writer shows how the toxic triangle develops and perpetuates itself in women.

Smashed: Story of a Drunken Girlhood by Koren Zalickas
Zalickas is an insightful and graceful writer whose memoir addresses the danger of alcohol dependence in girls and young women.

Happy Hours: Alcohol in a Woman's Life by Devin Jersild
A readable, personal treatment of women's relationship to alcohol, this book is filled with stories from women and sound advice about women's particular vulnerabilities—both social and physical—to alcohol.

DEPRESSION

Silencing the Self by Dana Crowley Jack
This breakthrough book describes how women's excessive concern with pleasing others and maintaining relationships leads them to sacrifice their own needs for the sake of their relationships.

Women and Depression by M. Sara Rosenthal
A straightforward guide by a medical health journalist, this book explains some of the theories of depression and describes the available treatments.

The Deepest Blue: How Women Face and Overcome Depression by Lauren Dockett
This work is a collection of stories about thirty women of all ages and backgrounds who are experiencing, or have recovered from, depression.

American Psychological Association (www.psych.org) and the Association for the Advancement of Behavioral Therapy (www.aabt.org)
These are both great resources if you feel you need to consult a psychiatrist or a psychologist but you don't know how to find one. Both of these Web sites also have information about depression, anxiety, and other mental health issues.

Memoirs

Speaking of Sadness: Depression, Disconnection, and the Meanings of Illness by David A. Karp
Karp uses his own experiences with battling depression to address the psychological, chemical, and social implications of the disease—and to give possible solutions.

You Are Not Alone: Words of Experience and Hope from the Journey through Depression by Julia Thorne
A valuable resource in combating the isolation that depression sufferers often feel, this book collects the reminiscences and support tips of both patients and doctors who have dealt with depression.

The Beast: A Journey through Depression by Tracy Thompson
Journalist Thompson chronicles her lifelong battle with depression in this frank, affecting memoir.

MEDITATION

Wherever You Go, There You Are by Jon Kabat-Zinn
This national bestseller provides hundreds of exercises for using meditation techniques in everyday life to become more calm, centered, and aware of your surroundings. It is written by one of the leading teachers of meditation techniques for psychotherapy purposes.

Full Catastrophe Living: Using the Wisdom of Your Body and Mind to Face Stress, Pain, and Illness by Jon Kabat-Zinn
Dr. Jon Kabat-Zinn developed a program of therapy using meditation techniques to help patients facing severe stress, physical pain, and medical illness. The program is the basis for several of the strategies suggested in *Women Conquering Depression*.

Mindfulness-Based Cognitive Therapy for Depression: A New Approach to Preventing Relapse by Zindel V. Segal, J. Mark G. Williams, and John Teasdale
This book outlines a new program of therapy for people with recurrent depressions that combines meditation techniques with cognitive therapy. This mindfulness-based approach has been shown to help in preventing relapse into depression, and is the basis for several of the techniques described in *Women Conquering Depression*.

Calming Your Anxious Mind: How Mindfulness and Compassion Can Free You from Anxiety, Fear, and Panic by Jeffrey Brantley
This book proposes techniques of mindfulness to relieve a wide range of stress-related conditions and to help develop skills for calming and relaxing the mind and body.

The Tao of Sobriety: Helping You to Recover from Alcohol and Drug Addiction by David Gregson, Jay S. Efran, and G. Alan Marlatt
This workbook provides exercises that combine meditation techniques with more traditional psychotherapy techniques to help people overcome alcohol and drug addiction.

YOUNG WOMEN AND THE TOXIC TRIANGLE

Reviving Ophelia: Saving the Selves of Adolescent Girls by Mary Pipher
This classic book tells the stories of several adolescent girls that therapist Mary
Pipher treated for eating disorders, depression, and drug abuse. Pipher makes
persuasive arguments about how the cultural message girls receive in early adolescence sets them up for the toxic triangle.

Girl in the Mirror: Mothers and Daughters in the Years of Adolescence by Nancy L.
Snyderman and Peg Streep
The authors offer tools for building openness, trust, and respect in adolescent
daughters, along with specific guides to dealing with difficult situations and
handling change. This is a wonderful resource for mothers.

*Queen Bees and Wannabes: Helping Your Daughter Survive Cliques, Gossip,
Boyfriends, and Other Realities of Adolescence* by Rosalind Wiseman
This book offers parents a guide to the often-mysterious world of adolescence.
Casting herself as a translator of "Girl World," Wiseman helps parents under-
stand their daughters' social lives, insecurities, and challenges.

The Young Women's Health Page (onsu.edu/library/teenhealth)
This user-friendly site provides information and resources for young women's
mental and physical health issues.

Adios Barbie (www.adiosbarbie.com)
Devoted to promoting self-esteem and a good body image by protesting negative and distorted images of women in the media, this site provides an interactive forum for young women to discuss weight-related pressures and
vulnerabilities.

Memoir

I Never Promised You a Rose Garden by Joanne Greenberg
This story of one girl's struggle with depression is touching and sympathetic—a
great resource for a young woman.

Notes

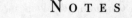

ONE: The Toxic Triangle

1. M. E. P. Seligman, R. Walker, and D. R. Rosenhan, *Abnormal Psychology* (New York: W.W. Norton, 2001).

2. G. L. Klerman and M. M. Weissman, "Increasing Rates of Depression," *Journal of the American Medical Association* 261 (1989): 2229–35. See also P. M. Lewinsohn, P. Rohde, J. R. Seeley, and S. A. Fischer, "Age-Cohort Changes in the Lifetime Occurrence of Depression and Other Mental Disorders," *Journal of Abnormal Psychology* 102 (1993): 110–20.

3. K. R. Jamison, *An Unquiet Mind: A Memoir of Moods and Madness* (New York: Knopf, 1995), p. 110.

4. R. C. Kessler, K. A. McGonagle, S. Zhao, et al., "Lifetime and 12-Month Prevalence of DSM-III-R Psychiatric Disorders in the United States, *Archives of General Psychiatry* 51 (1994): 8–19.

5. P. M. Lewinsohn, J. R. Seeley, K. C. Moerk, and R. H. Striegel-Moore, "Gender Differences in Eating Disorder Symptoms in Young Adults," *International Journal of Eating Disorders* 32 (2002): 426–40.

6. The men in this study were much less likely than the women to say they eat or binge eat to cope with distress: 13 percent said they eat and 5 percent said they binge eat.

7. R.C. Hawkins, S. Turrell, and L.J. Jackson, "Desirable and Undesirable Masculine and Feminine Traits in Relation to Students' Dieting Tendencies and Body-Image Dissatisfaction," *Sex Roles* 9 (1983): 705–18.

8. S.M. Dornbusch, J.M. Carlsmith, P.D. Duncan, et al., "Sexual Maturation, Social Class, and the Desire to Be Thin among Adolescent Females," *Developmental and Behavioral Pediatrics* 5 (1984): 308–14; J. Rierdan and E. Koff, "Depressive Symptomatology among Very Early Maturing Girls," *Journal of Youth and Adolescence* 20 (1991): 415–25; R.G. Simmons, D.A. Blyth, E.F. Van Cleave, and D.M. Bush, "Entry into Early Adolescence: The Impact of School Structure, Puberty, and Early Dating on Self-Esteem," *American Sociological Review* 44 (1979): 948–67; M. Tobin-Richards, A. Boxer, and A.C. Petersen, "The Psychological Significance of Pubertal Change: Sex Differences in Perception of Self during Early Adolescence," in *Girls at Puberty: Biological and Psychosocial Perspectives*, ed. J. Brooks-Gunn and A.C. Petersen (New York: Plenum, 1983), pp. 127–54.

9. Adapted from S. Nolen-Hoeksema, *Abnormal Psychology*, 3rd ed. (Boston: McGraw-Hill, 2004), p. 517.

10. *Diagnostic and Statistical Manual of Mental Disorders,* 4th ed., rev. (Washington, D.C.: American Psychiatric Association, 2000).

11. S. Nolen-Hoeksema, E. Stice, E. Wade, and C. Bohon, "Reciprocal Relations between Rumination and Bulimic, Substance Abuse, and Depressive Symptoms in Adolescent Females," forthcoming, 2005.

12. For reviews of these studies, see S. Lyubomirsky and C. Tkach, "The Consequences of Dysphoric Rumination," in *Depressive Rumination: Nature, Theory, and Treatment of Negative Thinking in Depression*, ed. C. Papageorgiou and A. Wells (New York: John Wiley, 2004), pp. 21–42; S. Nolen-Hoeksema, "The Response Styles Theory," in ibid., pp. 107–23.

13. M. McCarthy, "The Thin Ideal, Depression, and Eating Disorders in Women," *Behavioral Research and Therapy* 28 (1990): 205–18.

14. E. Stice, K. Presnell, and D. Spangler, "Risk Factors for Binge Eating Onset in Adolescent Girls: A 2-Year Prospective Investigation," *Health Psychology* 21 (2002): 131–38.

15. S. Nolen-Hoeksema and Z.A. Harrell, "Rumination, Depression, and Alcohol Use: Tests of Gender Differences," *Journal of Cognitive Psychotherapy* 16 (2002): 391–403.

16. P. Rohde, P.M. Lewinsohn, and J.R. Seeley, "Comorbidity of Unipolar Depression: II. Comorbidity with Other Mental Disorders in Adolescents and Adults," *Journal of Abnormal Psychology* 100 (1991): 214–22.

two: *Just How Toxic the Triangle Is*

1. P. M. Lewinsohn, P. Rohde, and J. R. Seeley, "The Clinical Consequences of Comorbidity," *Journal of the American Academy of Child and Adolescent Psychiatry* 34 (1995): 510–20.

2. E. Stice, K. Presnell, and D. Spangler, "Risk Factors for Binge Eating Onset in Adolescent Girls: A 2-Year Prospective Investigation," *Health Psychology* 21 (2002): 131–38.

3. E. Stice and C. G. Fairburn, "Dietary and Dietary-Depressive Subtypes of Bulimia Nervosa Show Differential Symptom Presentation, Social Impairment, Comorbidity, and Course of Illness," *Journal of Consulting and Clinical Psychology* 71 (2003): 1090–94.

4. P. M. Lewinsohn, R. H. Striegel-Moore, and J. R. Seeley, "Epidemiology and Natural Course of Eating Disorders in Young Women from Adolescence to Young Adulthood," *Journal of the American Academy of Child and Adolescent Psychiatry* 39 (2000): 1284–92.; R. H. Striegel-Moore, J. R. Seeley, and P. M. Lewinsohn, "Psychosocial Adjustment in Young Adulthood of Women Who Experienced an Eating Disorder during Adolescence," *Journal of the American Academy of Child and Adolescent Psychiatry* 42 (2003): 587–93.

5. S. E. Daley, C. Hammen, J. Davila, and D. Burge, "Axis II Symptomatology, Depression, and Life Stress during the Transition from Adolescence to Adulthood," *Journal of Consulting and Clinical Psychology* 66 (1998): 595–603.

6. A. Abbey, L. T. Ross, D. McDuffie, and P. McAuslan, "Alcohol and Dating Risk Factors for Sexual Assault among College Women," *Psychology of Women Quarterly* 20 (1996): 147–69.

7. J. R. Haber and T. Jacob, "Marital Interactions of Male versus Female Alcoholics," *Family Process* 36 (1997): 385–402.

8. R. C. Kessler, P. Berglund, O. Demler, et al., "The Epidemiology of Major Depressive Disorder: Results from the National Comorbidity Survey Replication (NCS-R)," *JAMA: Journal of the American Medical Association* 289 (2003): 3095–105.

9. M. Frezza, C. DiPadova, G. Pozzato, et al., "High Blood Alcohol Levels in Women: The Role of Decreased Gastric Alcohol Dehydrogenase Activity and First-Pass Metabolism," *New England Journal of Medicine* 322 (1990): 95–99.

10. S. B. Blume and M. Russell, "Alcohol and Substance Abuse in Obstetrics and Gynecology Practice," in *Psychological Aspects of Women's Health Care: The Interface between Psychiatry and Obstetrics and Gynecology,* 2nd ed., ed. N. L. Stotland (Washington, D.C.: American Psychiatric Press, 2001), pp. 421–39;

J. Gill, "The Effects of Moderate Alcohol Consumption on Female Hormone Levels and Reproductive Function," *Alcohol and Alcoholism* 35 (2000): 417–23; A. D. Klassen and S. C. Wilsnack, "Sexual Experience and Drinking among Women in a U.S. National Survey," *Archives of Sexual Behavior* 15 (1986): 363–92.

11. E. Z. Hanna, S. P. Chou, and B. F. Grant, "The Relationship between Drinking and Heart Disease Morbidity in the United States: Results from the National Health Interview Survey," *Alcoholism: Clinical and Experimental Research* 21 (1997): 111–18.

12. D. M. Dougherty, J. M. Bjork, and R. H. Bennett, "Effects of Alcohol on Rotary Pursuit Performance: A Gender Comparison," *The Psychological Record* 48 (1998): 393–405; S. J. Nixon, "Cognitive Deficits in Alcoholic Women," *Alcohol Health and Research World* 18 (1994): 228–32.

13. J. Polivy and C. P. Herman, "Causes of Eating Disorders," *Annual Review of Psychology* 53 (2002): 182–213.

14. N. Schneiderman, G. Ironson, and S. D. Siegel, "Stress and Health: Psychological, Behavioral, and Biological Determinants," *Annual Review of Clinical Psychology* 1 (2005): 607–28.

15. L. L. Judd and H. S. Akiskal, "Delineating the Longitudinal Structure of Depressive Illness: Beyond Clinical Subtypes and Duration Thresholds," *Pharmacopsychiatry* 33 (2000): 3–7; L. Judd, H. Akiskal, J. Maser, et al., "A Prospective 12-Year Study of Subsyndromal and Syndromal Depressive Symptoms in Unipolar Major Depressive Disorders," *Archives of General Psychiatry* 55 (1998): 694–700.

16. C. G. Fairburn, Z. Cooper, H. A. Doll, et al., "The Natural Course of Bulimia Nervosa and Binge-Eating Disorder in Young Women," *Archives of General Psychiatry* 57 (2000): 659–65; B. Herpertz-Dahlmann, B. Muller, S. Herpertz, and N. Heussen, "Prospective 10-Year Follow-Up in Adolescent Anorexia Nervosa—Course, Outcome, Psychiatric Morbidity, and Psychosocial Adaptation," *Journal of Child Psychology and Psychiatry* 42 (2001): 603–12.

17. R. C. Kessler, M. Olfson, and P. A. Berglund, "Patterns and Predictors of Treatment Contact after the First Onset of Psychiatric Disorders," *American Journal of Psychiatry* 155 (1998): 62–68; R. C. Kessler, P. Berglund, O. Demler, et al., "The Epidemiology of Major Depressive Disorder: Results from the National Comorbidity Survey Replication (NCS-R)," *JAMA: Journal of the American Medical Association* 289 (2003): 3095–105.

18. R. J. Boland and M. B. Keller, "Course and Outcome of Depression," in *Handbook of Depression,* ed. I. H. Gotlib and C. L. Hammen (New York: Guil-

ford Press, 2002), pp. 43–60; T. E. Joiner, Jr., "Depression in Its Interpersonal Context," in ibid., pp. 295–313.

19. D. A. Cole, J. M. Martin, L. G. Peeke, et al., "Are Cognitive Errors of Underestimation Predictive or Reflective of Depressive Symptoms in Children? A Longitudinal Study," *Journal of Abnormal Psychology* 107 (1998): 481–96; S. Nolen-Hoeksema, J. S. Girgus, and M. E. P. Seligman, "Predictors and Consequences of Depressive Symptoms in Children: A 5-Year Longitudinal Study," *Journal of Abnormal Psychology* 101 (1992): 405–22.

THREE: *A Woman's Place*

1. For academic reviews of the literature covered in this section, see N. R. Crick and C. Zahn-Waxler, "The Development of Psychopathology in Females and Males: Current Progress and Future Challenges," *Development and Psychopathology* 15 (2003): 719–42; K. Keenan and D. S. Shaw, "Starting at the Beginning: Exploring the Etiology of Antisocial Behavior in the First Years of Life," in *Causes of Conduct Disorder and Juvenile Delinquency,* ed. B. B. Lahey, T. E. Moffitt, et al. (New York: Guilford Press, 2003), pp. 153–81; S. Nolen-Hoeksema, "The Response Styles Theory," in *Depressive Rumination: Nature, Theory, and Treatment of Negative Thinking in Depression*, ed. C. Papageorgiou and A. Wells (New York: Wiley, 2004), pp. 107–23; S. Nolen-Hoeksema and J. S. Girgus, "The Emergence of Gender Differences in Depression in Adolescence," *Psychological Bulletin* 115 (1994): 424–43.

2. H. Hops, "Intergenerational Transmission of Depressive Symptoms: Gender and Developmental Considerations," in *Interpersonal Factors in the Origin and Course of Affective Disorders*, ed. C. Mudt and M. J. Goldstein (London: Gaskell/Royal College of Psychiatrists, 1996), pp. 113–29.

3. S. Nolen-Hoeksema and C. Rusting, "Gender Differences in Well-Being," in *Foundations of Hedonic Psychology: Scientific Perspectives on Enjoyment and Suffering*, ed. D. Kahneman, E. Diener, and N. Schwarz (New York: Russell Sage Foundation, 1999), pp. 330–52.

4. C. Rusting and S. Nolen-Hoeksema, "Regulating Responses to Anger: Effects of Rumination and Distraction on Angry Mood," *Journal of Personality and Social Psychology* 74 (1998): 790–803.

5. L. D. Butler and S. Nolen-Hoeksema, "Gender Differences in Responses to a Depressed Mood in a College Sample," *Sex Roles* 30 (1994): 331–46.

6. S. Nolen-Hoeksema and B. Jackson, "Mediators of the Gender Difference in Rumination," *Psychology of Women Quarterly* 25 (2001): 37–47.

7. H. Bruch, *Eating Disorders: Obesity, Anorexia Nervosa, and the Person Within* (New York: Basic Booksl, 1973).

8. S. Nolen-Hoeksema, *Abnormal Psychology,* 4th ed. (Boston: McGraw-Hill, 2006). In press.

9. J. Polivy and C. P. Herman, "Causes of Eating Disorders," *Annual Review of Psychology* 53 (2002): 182–213.

10. A. J. Hill and J. A. Franklin, "Mothers, Daughters, and Dieting: Investigating the Transmission of Weight Control," *British Journal of Clinical Psychology* 37 (1998): 3–13.

11. T. Jacob and D. A. Bremer, "Assortative Mating among Men and Women Alcoholics," *Journal of Studies on Alcohol* 47 (1986): 219–22.; L. J. Roberts and K. E. Leonard, "Gender Differences and Similarities in the Alcohol and Marriage Relationship," in *Gender and Alcohol: Individual and Social Perspectives*, ed. R. W. Wilsnack and S. C. Wilsnack (Piscataway, N.J.: Rutgers Center of Alcohol Studies, 1997), pp. 289–311.

12. A. Young, personal communication, April 12, 2005.

13. C. V. Wiseman, J. J. Gray, J. E. Morrison, and A. H. Ahrens, "Cultural Expectations of Thinness in Women: An Update," *International Journal of Eating Disorders* 11 (1992): 85–89.

14. R. F. Guy, B. A. Rankin, and M. J. Norvell, "The Relation of Sex Role Stereotyping to Body Image," *Journal of Psychology* 105 (1980): 167–73; B. J. Rolls, I. C. Fedoroff, and J. F. Guthrie, "Gender Differences in Eating Behavior and Body Weight Regulation," *Health Psychology* 10 (1991): 133–42.

15. D. Mori, S. Chaiken, and P. Pliner, " 'Eating Lightly' and the Self-Presentation of Femininity," *Journal of Personality and Social Psychology* 53 (1987): 693–702; P. Pliner and S. Chaiken, "Eating, Social Motives, and Self-Presentation in Women and Men," *Journal of Experimental Social Psychology* 26 (1990): 240–54.

16. E. Stice, "Risk and Maintenance Factors for Eating Pathology: A Meta-analytic Review," *Psychological Bulletin* 128 (2002): 825–48.

17. E. Stice and H. Shaw, "Adverse Effects of the Media-Portrayed Thin-Ideal on Women, and Linkages to Bulimic Symptomatology," *Journal of Social and Clinical Psychology* 13 (1994): 288–308.

18. E. Stice, D. Spangler, and W. S. Agras, "Exposure to Media-Portrayed Thin-Ideal Images Adversely Affects Vulnerable Girls: A Longitudinal Experiment," *Journal of Social and Clinical Psychology* 20 (2001): 271–89.

19. E. Stice, J. Maxfield, and T. Wells, "Adverse Effects of Social Pressure to Be Thin on Young Women: An Experimental Investigation of the Effects of 'Fat Talk,' " *International Journal of Eating Disorders* 34 (2003): 108–17. They

also had a second accomplice, who was twenty years old, 5 foot 9 inches tall, and 126 pounds.

20. M. L. Granner, D. R. Black, and D. A. Abood, "Levels of Cigarette and Alcohol Use Related to Eating-Disorder Attitudes," *American Journal of Health Behavior* 26 (2002): 43–55.

21. E. Stice, E. M. Burton, and H. Shaw, "Prospective Relations between Bulimic Pathology, Depression, and Substance Abuse: Unpacking Comorbidity in Adolescent Girls," *Journal of Consulting and Clinical Psychology* 72 (2004): 62–71.

22. B. L. Fredrickson and T. A. Roberts, "Objectification Theory: Toward Understanding Women's Lived Experiences and Mental Health Risks," *Psychology of Women Quarterly* 21 (1997): 173–206.

FOUR: *Our Bodies Conspire against Us*

1. C. O. Ladd, R. L. Huot, K. V. Thrivikraman, et al., "Long-Term Behavioral and Neuroendocrine Adaptations to Adverse Early Experience," *Progress in Brain Research* 122 (2000): 81–103.

2. D. Cicchetti and S. L. Toth, "Child Maltreatment," *Annual Review of Clinical Psychology* 1 (2005): 409–38.

3. C. Heim, P. M. Plotsky, and C. B. Nemeroff, "Importance of Studying the Contributions of Early Adverse Experience to Neurobiological Findings in Depression," *Neuropsychopharmacology* 29 (2004): 641–48.

4. C. Heim, D. J. Newport, D. Wagner, et al., "The Role of Early Adverse Experience and Adulthood Stress in the Prediction of Neuroendocrine Stress Reactivity in Women: A Multiple Regression Analysis," *Depression and Anxiety* 15 (2002): 117–25.

5. Heim et al., see note 3.

6. J. D. Bremner, M. Vythilingam, G. Anderson, et al., "Assessment of the Hypothalamic-Pituitary-Adrenal Axis over a 24-Hour Diurnal Period and in Response to Neuroendocrine Challenges in Women with and without Childhood Sexual Abuse and Posttraumatic Stress Disorder," *Biological Psychiatry* 54 (2003): 710–18; M. Vythilingam, C. Heim, J. Newport, et al., "Childhood Trauma Associated with Smaller Hippocampal Volume in Women with Major Depression," *American Journal of Psychiatry* 159 (2002): 2072–80.

7. C. B. Nemeroff, C. M. Heim, M. E. Thase, et al., "Differential Responses to Psychotherapy versus Pharmacotherapy in Patients with Chronic Forms of Major Depression and Childhood Trauma," *Proceedings of the National Academy of Science,* November 13, 2003.

8. H. S. Mayberg, "Modulating Dysfunctional Limbic-Cortical Circuits in

Depression: Towards Development of Brain-Based Algorithms for Diagnosis and Optimized Treatment," *British Medical Bulletin* 65 (2003): 193–207. Interestingly, patients who respond to cognitive therapy show different brain changes than patients who respond best to drug treatments.

9. J. Kaufman, P. Plotsky, C. Nemeroff, et al., "Effects of Early Adverse Experiences on Brain Structure and Function: Clinical Implications," *Biological Psychiatry* 48 (2000): 778–90.

10. K. S. Kendler, C. G. Davis, and R. C. Kessler, "The Familial Aggregation of Common Psychiatric and Substance Use Disorders in the National Comorbidity Survey: A Family History Study," *British Journal of Psychiatry* 179 (1997): 541–48.

11. K. S. Kendler, C. MacLean, M. Neale, et al., "The Genetic Epidemiology of Bulimia Nervosa," *American Journal of Psychiatry* 148 (1991): 1627–37.

12. K. S. Kendler, A. C. Heath, M. C. Neale, et al., "A Population-Based Twin Study of Alcoholism in Women," *JAMA: Journal of the American Medical Association* 268 (1992): 1877–82.

13. K. S. Kendler and C. A. Prescott, "A Population-Based Twin Study of Lifetime Major Depression in Men and Women," *Archives of General Psychiatry* 56 (1999): 39–44.

14. R. Rowe, A. Pickles, E. Simonoff, et al., "Bulimic Symptoms in the Virginia Twin Study of Adolescent Behavioral Development: Correlates, Comorbidity, and Genetics," *Biological Psychiatry* 51 (2002): 172–82.

15. K. S. Kendler, "Twin Studies of Psychiatric Illness: Current Status and Future Directions," *Archives of General Psychiatry* 50 (1993): 905–15.

16. C. M. Grilo, R. Sinha, and S. S. O'Malley, "Eating Disorders and Alcohol Use Disorders," *Alcohol Research and Health* 26 (2002): 151–60.

17. For example, K. S. Kendler, E. E. Walters, M. C. Neale, et al., "The Structure of Genetic and Environmental Risk Factors for Six Major Psychiatric Disorders in Women," *Archives of General Psychiatry* 52 (1995): 374–83; K. M. von Ranson, M. McGue, and W. G. Iacono, "Disordered Eating and Substance Use in an Epidemiological Sample: II. Associations within Families," *Psychology of Addictive Behaviors* 17 (2003): 193–202.

18. A. Caspi, K. Sugden, T. E. Moffitt, et al., "Influence of Life Stress on Depression: Moderation by a Polymorphism in the 5-HTT Gene," *Science* 301 (2003): 386–89.

19. M. E. Thase, R. Jindal, and R. H. Howland, "Biological Aspects of Depression," in *Handbook of Depression*, ed. I. H. Gotlib and C. L. Hammen (New York: Guilford Press, 2002), pp. 192–218.

20. J. E. Mitchell and M. deZwaan, "Pharmacological Treatments of Binge

Eating," in *Binge Eating: Nature, Assessment and Treatment*, ed. C. E. Fairburn and G. T. Wilson (New York: Guilford Press, 1993), pp. 250–69.

21. G. K. Frank, W. H. Kaye, T. E. Weltzin, et al., "Altered Response to Meta-Chlorophenylpiperazine in Anorexia Nervosa: Support for a Persistent Alteration of Serotonin Activity after Short-Term Weight Restoration," *International Journal of Eating Disroders* 30 (2001): 57–68.

22. J. J. Mann, D. A. Brent, and V. Arango, "The Neurobiology and Genetics of Suicide and Attempted Suicide: A Focus on the Serotonergic System," *Neuropsychopharmacology* 24 (2001): 467–77.

23. K. C. Berridge and E. S. Valenstein, "What Psychological Process Mediates Feeding Evoked by Electrical Stimulation of the Lateral Hypothalamus?" *Behavioral Neuroscience* 105 (1991): 3–14.

24. E. Stice, "Risk and Maintenance Factors for Eating Pathology: A Meta-analytic Review," *Psychological Bulletin* 128 (2002): 825–48.

25. M. E. Keck, T. Welt, M. B. Muller, et al., "Repetitive Transcranial Magnetic Stimulation Increases the Release of Dopamine in the Mesolimbic and Mesostriatal System," *Neuropharmacology* 43 (2002): 101–10.

26. W. W. Ishak, M. H. Rapaport, and J. G. Gotto, "Emerging Treatment Options in Treatment-Resistant Depression and Anxiety Disorders," *CNS Spectrums* 9 (2004): 25–32.

27. J. M. Twenge and S. Nolen-Hoeksema, "Age, Gender, Race, SES, and Birth Cohort Differences on the Children's Depression Inventory: A Meta-analysis," *Journal of Abnormal Psychology* 111 (2002): 578–88.

28. A. Angold, E. J. Costello, A. Erkanli, and C. M. Worthman, "Pubertal Change in Hormones of Adolescent Girls," *Psychological Medicine* 29 (1999): 1043–53.

29. M. Steiner, E. Dunn, and L. Born, "Hormones and Mood: From Menarche to Menopause and Beyond," *Journal of Affective Disorders* 74 (2003): 67–83.

30. E. Young and A. Korzun, "Psychoneuroendocrinology of Depression: Hypothalamic-Pituitary-Gonadal Axis," *Psychiatric Clinics of North America* 21 (1998): 309–23.

31. J. Silberg, A. Pickles, M. Rutter, et al., "The Influence of Genetic Factors and Life Stress on Depression among Adolescent Girls," *Archives of General Psychiatry* 56 (1999): 225–32.

32. A. Caspi and T. Moffitt, "Individual Differences Are Accentuated during Periods of Social Change: The Sample Case of Girls at Puberty," *Journal of Personality and Social Psychology* 61 (1991): 157–68; J. A. Graber, P. M. Lewinsohn, J. R. Seeley, and J. Brooks-Gunn, "Is Psychopathology Associated with the Timing of Pubertal Development?" *Journal of the American Academy of Child*

and Adolescent Psychiatry 36 (1997): 1768–76; C. Hayward, J. D. Killen, D. M. Wilson, and L. D. Hammer, "Psychiatric Risk Associated with Early Puberty in Adolescent Girls," *Journal of the American Academy of Child and Adolescent Psychiatry* 36 (1997): 255–62.

33. J. Rierdan and E. Koff, "Depressive Symptomatology among Very Early Maturing Girls," *Journal of Youth and Adolescence* 20 (1991): 415–25.

34. B. Allgood-Merten, P. M. Lewinsohn, and H. Hops, "Sex Differences and Adolescent Depression," *Journal of Abnormal Psychology* 99 (1990): 55–63.

35. A. C. Petersen, P. A. Sarigiani, and R. E. Kennedy, "Adolescent Depression: Why More Girls?" *Journal of Youth and Adolescence* 20 (1991): 247–71.

36. R. G. Simmons and D. A. Blyth, *Moving into Adolescence: The Impact of Pubertal Change and School Context* (New York: Aldine de Gruyter, 1987).

37. J. M. Cyranowski, E. Frank, E. Young, and M. K. Shear, "Adolescent Onset of the Gender Difference in Lifetime Rates of Major Depression: A Theoretical Model," *Archives of General Psychiatry* 57 (2000): 21–27.

FIVE: *Thinking Our Way into the Toxic Triangle*

1. For a review of this work, see S. Nolen-Hoeksema, *Women Who Think Too Much: How to Break Free of Overthinking and Reclaim Your Life* (New York: Henry Holt, 2003); and S. Nolen-Hoeksema, "Further Evidence for the Role of Psychosocial Factors in Depression Chronicity," *Clinical Psychology: Science and Practice* 7 (2000): 224–27.

2. S. Lyubomirsky and S. Nolen-Hoeksema, "Effects of Self-Focused Rumination on Negative Thinking and Interpersonal Problem-Solving," *Journal of Personality and Social Psychology* 69 (1995): 176–90.

3. S. Nolen-Hoeksema and C. G. Davis, " 'Thanks for Sharing That': Ruminators and Their Social Support Networks," *Journal of Personality and Social Psychology* 77 (1999): 801–14.

4. S. Nolen-Hoeksema and B. Jackson, "Mediators of the Gender Difference in Rumination," *Psychology of Women Quarterly* 25 (2001): 37–47.

5. For an excellent discussion of all-or-nothing thinking, see D. Burns, *Feeling Good: The New Mood Therapy* (New York: Morrow, 1980).

6. J. Polivy and C. P. Herman, "Causes of Eating Disorders," *Annual Review of Psychology* 53 (2002): 182–213.

7. G. A. Marlatt, *Harm Reduction: Pragmatic Strategies for Managing High-Risk Behaviors* (New York: Guilford Press, 1998).

8. J. Crocker and C. Wolfe, "Contingencies of Self-Worth," *Psychological Review* 108 (2001): 593–628.

9. C. Power, J. Crocker, and R. Luhtanen, "The Ups and Downs of Appearance: Appearance-Contingent Self-Worth and Gendered Psychological Well-Being" (unpublished).

10. K. D. Vohs, Z. R. Voelz, J. W. Pettit, et al., "Perfectionism, Body Dissatisfaction, and Self-Esteem: An Interactive Model of Bulimic Symptom Development," *Journal of Social and Clinical Psychology* 20 (2001): 476–97; K. D. Vohs, A. M. Bardone, T. E. Joiner, Jr., et al., "Perfectionism, Perceived Weight Status, and Self-Esteem Interact to Predict Bulimic Symptoms: A Model of Bulimic Symptom Development," *Journal of Abnormal Psychology* 108 (1999): 695–700.

11. R. K. Luhtanen and J. Crocker, "Fragile Self-Esteem and Alcohol Use in College Students," *Psychology of Addictive Behaviors* (in press).

12. J. T. Sargent and J. Crocker, "Contingencies of Self-Worth and Depressive Symptoms in College Students" (under review).

SIX: *Transforming Vulnerabilities into Strengths*

1. Z. V. Segal, J. M. G. Williams, and J. D. Teasdale, *Mindfulness-Based Cognitive Therapy for Depression* (New York: Guilford Press, 2002).

2. G. A. Marlatt, K. Witkiewitz, T. M. Dillworth, et al., "Vipassana Meditation as a Treatment for Alcohol and Drug Use Disorders," in *Mindfulness and Acceptance: Expanding the Cognitive-Behavioral Tradition*, ed. S. C. Hayes, V. M. Follette, and M. M. Linehan (New York: Guilford Press, 2004), pp. 261–87.

3. Marlatt et al., see note 2.

4. Segal et al., see note 1.

5. G. A. Marlatt and J. R. Gordon, eds., *Relapse Prevention* (New York: Guilford Press, 1985); R. Kadden, K. Carroll, D. Donovan, et al., *Cognitive-Behavioral Coping Skills Therapy Manual* (Washington, D.C.: National Institute on Alcohol Abuse and Alcoholism, 1995).

6. Kabat-Zinn, *Wherever You Go, There You Are: Mindfulness Meditation in Everyday Life* (New York: Hyperion, 1994).

7. Marlatt et al., see note 2.

8. Kadden et al., see note 5.

9. C. G. Fairburn, *Overcoming Binge Eating* (New York: Guilford Press, 1995).

10. J. Polivy and C. P. Herman, "Causes of Eating Disorders," *Annual Review of Psychology* 53 (2002): 182–213.

SEVEN: *Moving toward a Healthier You*

1. E. L. Deci and R. M. Ryan, "A Motivational Approach to Self: Integration in Personality," in *Nebraska Symposium on Motivation*, ed. R. Dienstbier (Lincoln: University of Nebraska Press, 1991), pp. 237–88.

2. L. L. Martin and A. Tesser, "Some Ruminative Thoughts," in *Ruminative Thoughts*, ed. R. S. Wyer, Jr. (Mahwah, N.J.: Erlbaum Associates, 1996), pp. 1–48.

3. Excerpted from S. Nolen-Hoeksema, *Women Who Think Too Much: How to Break Free of Overthinking and Reclaim Your Life* (New York: Henry Holt, 2003).

4. I can only cover so much in one book, but several self-help books specific to one of the three sides of the toxic triangle provide even more ideas for positive change. For changing eating-related behaviors, I recommend Dr. Christopher Fairburn's *Overcoming Binge Eating* (1995). For drinking-related behaviors, have a look at *The Tao of Sobriety: Helping You to Recover from Alcohol and Drug Addiction* (2002), by psychologists David Gregson, Jay Efran, and Alan Marlatt. For depression and overthinking, consult my book *Women Who Think Too Much: How to Break Free from Overthinking and Reclaim Your Life* (2003) and Dr. David Burns's *Feeling Good: The New Mood Therapy* (1999).

5. S. Nolen-Hoeksema, "The Response Styles Theory," in *Depressive Rumination: Nature, Theory, and Treatment of Negative Thinking in Depression*, ed. C. Papageorgiou and A. Wells (New York: Wiley, 2004), pp. 107–23.

6. A. M. Nezu, T. J. D'Zurilla, L. Marni, and C. M. Nezu, "Problem-Solving Therapy for Adults," in *Social Problem Solving: Theory, Research, and Training*, ed. E. C. Chang, T. J. D'Zurilla, L. J. Sanna (Washington, D.C.: American Psychological Association, 2004), pp. 171–91.

7. M. E. McCullough, "Forgiveness as Human Strength: Theory, Measurement, and Links to Well-Being," *Journal of Social and Clinical Psychology* 19 (2000): 43–55; M. E. McCullough, "Forgiveness: Who Does It and How Do They Do It?" *Current Directions in Psychological Science* 10 (2001): 194–97.

8. G. A. Marlatt and J. R. Gordon, eds., *Relapse Prevention* (New York: Guilford Press, 1985).

EIGHT: *Channeling Our Daughters' Strengths*

1. For example, see E. Stice and H. Shaw, "Eating Disorder Prevention Programs: A Meta-Analytic Review," *Psychological Bulletin* 130 (2004): 206–27.

2. J. M. Cyranowski, E. Frank, E. Young, and M. K. Shear, "Adolescent Onset of the Gender Difference in Lifetime Rates of Major Depression: A Theoretical Model," *Archives of General Psychiatry* 57 (2000): 21–27.

3. A. E. Fruzzetti and K. M. Iverson, "Mindfulness, Acceptance, Validation, and 'Individual' Psychopathology in Couples," in *Mindfulness and Acceptance: Expanding the Cognitive-Behavioral Tradition*, ed. S. C. Hayes, V. M. Follette, and M. M. Linehan (New York: Guilford Press, 2004).

4. E. Stice and J. Shaw, "Eating Disorder Prevention Programs," pp. 206–27; G. A. Marlatt, M. E. Larimer, J. S. Baer, and L. A. Quigley, "Harm Reduction for Alcohol Problems: Moving beyond the Controlled Drinking Economy," *Behavior Therapy* 24 (1993): 461–503; G. N. Clarke, W. Hawkins, M. Murphy, et al., "Targeted Prevention of Unipolar Depressive Disorder in an At-Risk Sample of High School Adolescents: A Randomized Trial of a Group Cognitive Intervention," *Journal of the American Academy of Child and Adolescent Psychiatry* 34 (1995): 312–21.

5. S. Nolen-Hoeksema and J. Morrow, "Effects of Rumination and Distraction on Naturally Occurring Depressed Mood," *Cognition and Emotion* 7 (1993): 561–70.

6. G. A. Marlatt, J. S. Baer, and M. Larimer, "Preventing Alcohol Abuse in College Students: A Harm Reduction Approach," in *Alcohol Problems among Adolescents: Current Directions in Prevention Research*, ed. G. M. Boyd, J. Joward, and R. A. Zucker (Hillsdale, N.J.: L. Erlbaum, 1995), pp. 147–72.

7. G. A. Marlatt, J. S. Baer, D. R. Kivlahan, et al., "Screening and Brief Intervention for High-Risk College Student Drinkers: Results from a 2-Year Follow-Up Assessment," *Journal of Consulting and Clinical Psychology* 66 (1998): 604–15.

8. V. E. Frankl, *Man's Search for Meaning* (New York: Washington Square Press, 1963), p. 104.

9. A. Nafisi, *Reading Lolita in Tehran* (New York: Random House, 2003).

ACKNOWLEDGMENTS

━━━━━━━━━━▼━━━━━━━━━━

Women Conquering Depression is based on research I've conducted over the last twenty years with several students and colleagues, including Sonja Lyubomirsky, Judith Larson, Joan Girgus, Cheryl Rusting, Andrew Ward, Zaje Harrell, Benita Jackson, Barbara Fredrickson, Tomi-Ann Roberts, Robert Zucker, and Eric Stice. I thank them, and the thousands of women and men who have participated in our research, for their contributions. I also thank the National Institutes of Health and the William T. Grant Foundation for funding much of this research.

My sincere thanks go to Jennifer Barth of Henry Holt and Todd Shuster, my literary agent, for encouraging me to develop a book on the toxic triangle, and my deep appreciation to Vanessa

Mobley at Henry Holt for her skillful editorial guidance as I wrote this book.

As always, thank you to my family and friends for their abiding support of me and my work.

INDEX

$$\blacktriangledown$$

conditions of self-esteem and
all-or-nothing thinking and, 131
defined, xii, 1–5
entering, 25–31
eradicating, with our daughters, 223–25
escaping, 31–32
female hormones and, 101–5
fight-or-flight response malfunction
and, 91–92
gender roles, 61
genetics and, 95–97
industry and, 36–38
pathways into, 9–20
physical health and, 53–59
relationships and, 42–49
research on, 38–40
scars of, 58
self-focused coping and, 7–9
why we don't recognize, 5–6
trauma, early
overcoming, 91–92
scars of, 88–91
triggers
binges and, 156
helping daughter identify, 210
tuning into thoughts technique, 143–44
TV shows, 224
Twenge, Jean, 12
twin studies, 95–96, 102

undermining behavior, 182–87
unmitigated communion, 70–71
urge surfing, 145–46

values, pursuing deeply held, 178–79
violence, 47–49

Vohs, Kathleen, 131
volunteer work, 179
vulnerabilities, transforming, into
strengths, 133–35

weight
business and, 36
social pressure and, 79–80
Weissman, Myrna, 10
Wherever You Go, There You Are
(Kabat-Zinn), 147
Williams, Mark, 143
women
alcohol metabolism and, 30, 53
anger and, 65–67
female hormones and, 101–5
husband's drinking and, 77–79
physical harm of alcohol, 53–54
as relationship keepers, 67–79
self-focused coping and, 62–64
statistics on drinking, 17–18
suffering of, ignored, 35–38
Women Who Think Too Much, xi, 112, 211,
214
work lives, 58
writing
techniques, 195–96
worries, 214

yoga, 141, 150
Young, Amy, 79
yo-yo eating patterns, xii, 3

Zahn-Waxler, Carolyn, 67–68
Zoloft, 98
Zucker, Robert, 93

ABOUT THE AUTHOR

▼

SUSAN NOLEN-HOEKSEMA, PH.D., is a professor of psychology at Yale University. She has taught at Stanford University and the University of Michigan. She received her B.A. from Yale and her Ph.D. from the University of Pennsylvania. The author of *Women Who Think Too Much,* she has been conducting award-winning research on women's mental health for twenty years with funding from the National Institutes of Health, the National Science Foundation, and the William T. Grant Foundation. She was awarded the Leadership Award from the Committee on Women and the Early Career Award from the American Psychological Association. She lives near New Haven, Connecticut, with her husband, Richard, and her son, Michael.

Bestselling and award-winning psychologist
Susan Nolen-Hoeksema, Ph.D.,
gives women the tools and the insight
to lead balanced, fulfilling lives

Available from Holt Paperbacks

Women Who Think Too Much:
How to Break Free of Overthinking and Reclaim Your Life

In this self-help classic—called "groundbreaking" by *USA Today*—renowned psychologist Dr. Susan Nolen-Hoeksema delves into the problem of women's overthinking: the countless hours spent ruminating about negative ideas, feelings, and experiences that can lead to sadness, anxiety, and even depression. Drawing on her extensive studies in the area, Nolen-Hoeksema challenges the assumption that constantly expressing and analyzing emotions is a good thing, and offers concrete strategies and exercises that any woman can use to escape the overthinking cycle and live a more productive and rewarding life.

Women Conquering Depression:
How to Gain Control of Eating, Drinking, and
Overthinking and Embrace a Healthier Life

Depression is a common and debilitating problem among women, but it rarely occurs in a vacuum. As Dr. Nolen-Hoeksema's research shows, overthinking and depressive moods often coexist with unhealthy eating habits or heavy drinking. Filled with practical advice and coping strategies, this innovative book explains how any woman can break the cycle of eating, drinking, and overthinking in order to conquer depression and depressive thoughts, as well as regain emotional well-being, physical health, and a balance in relationships with family, friends, and work.

The Power of Women:
Harness Your Unique Strengths
at Home, at Work, and in Your Community

Drawing on original research and the inspiring and instructive stories of real women, Dr. Susan Nolen-Hoeksema identifies the skill sets that women—based on their biology and social roles—bring to challenges: mental strengths, such as the ability to manage scarce resources; identity strengths, which maintain strong values under pressure; emotional strengths, such as anticipating the effects of decisions; and relational strengths, with an emphasis on win-win solutions. Packed with hands-on assessments and exercises, this revolutionary book of self-improvement shows women how to hone their skills as entrepreneurs and managers, mothers and wives, mentors and community leaders—and as individuals pursuing their talents and dreams.